THE COMPLETE
New Zealand
Seafood COOKBOOK

The Auckland Seafood School

Photography by Sean Shadbolt

PENGUIN BOOKS

This cookbook is dedicated to the fishermen and fisherwomen who are now engaged in bringing fish to the Auckland Fish Market in new and exciting ways. This will not only allow New Zealanders to eat even fresher seafood but will also enhance the sustainability of the resources for the benefit of the children and grandchildren of the people of Auckland. The dedication and passion for the industry of these fishermen and fisherwomen is like no other. They are the keenest advocates for the protection of New Zealand's unique marine environment and the sustainable use and management of its resources.

Contents

Foreword 4

Introduction 6

About this cookbook 8

Where does your fish come from? 8

Fishing methods 9

Seafood industry information and sustainability 9

What is in seafood that makes it so good? 10

Catching, handling, purchasing and storing fish 11

Preparing fish and shellfish 12

Seafood cooking techniques 15

Kitchen essentials 17

Visual identification guide 20

Tapas and light tastes 30

Salads and light meals 56

Pasta, rice and noodles 108

Barbecues and grills 130

Pan-seared, deep-fried and sautéed 164

Pies, casseroles, bakes and steamed and one-pot meals 202

Soups, stocks and chowders 240

Basic recipes 258

Contributing chefs 274

Glossary 276

Index 278

Acknowledgements 288

'We are truly blessed to live in New Zealand, a land with a bountiful coast and a fishery subject to effective management policies.'

Foreword

I have an early and very vivid childhood memory of my father walking through the front door carrying a crayfish in each hand. Although he held them above his waist, their tails dragged on the ground. They were monstrous crustaceans, dark maroon in colour and almost as big as me – I was in awe!

Dad had just flown back from the Chatham Islands in a Sunderland Flying Boat and the crays were still fresh. Mum boiled the copper, which was also where our clothes were washed, and where the huge beasts had to be cooked one at a time. Mum added salt and a little mustard powder to the water – which is something I still do today.

Dad loved mussels too and there would be regular low-tide pilgrimages to the rocks at Taylors Mistake where he and his mates would tear sack-loads of mussels off the rocks. At home the preserving pan would come out and the mussels would be steamed open, then placed in preserving jars and marinated in vinegar.

Seafood was exactly that: food. Anything you could harvest meant less spent at the grocery store and more money for something else.

On the estuary in front of our shack we dragged for flounder, often taking so many that Dad and I would share the excess by taking them round to the neighbours in a wheelbarrow. There was never any thought given to sustainability – back then, the resource was somehow expected to be limitless. Now we

know differently, of course, because stocks of many species have come under serious threat. But Kiwis being Kiwis and great innovators, we developed a system called 'quota management'. This involves keeping enough of each species in the ocean to ensure that they will not only survive but actually thrive, and in the process allocate a quota. When the quota is caught, the target species gets a rest.

You will learn about the Quota Management System in the pages that follow and what you will also come to understand is that seafood has become much more than food on the table. It is now an art form! Chefs conjure, create and prepare all manner of piscatorial delights in ways that my parents would never have thought possible. We have come a long way with seafood, and the delicate flavours and textures deserve our profound respect.

Just like you, I have a passion for seafood and a desire to see our fisheries thrive. In many ways we are truly blessed to live in New Zealand, a land with a bountiful coast and a fishery subject to effective management policies. I strongly believe in our future, a future filled with further innovation, improved systems and succulent seafood.

Follow these recipes, innovate and share, and a world of culinary opportunity will open to you. Enjoy!

Graeme Sinclair
Television presenter and fishing expert

'We are incredibly privileged to be able to catch our own seafood in New Zealand – whether through fishing, diving or snorkelling.'

Introduction

From long summer family holidays spent in the campground at Ohope beach back in the '70s, to diving and fishing off the coastline of Great Barrier Island in recent times, my life has always been consumed by the New Zealand coast and its amazing waters. I am the manager of the Auckland Seafood School, a cooking school based at the Auckland Fish Market. The school was opened by Sanford Limited in June 2004 to encourage the incorporation of seafood into everyday meals, making use of the variety of species available in New Zealand waters and from your local food store or fish market. Located on the first floor of the Auckland Fish Market, the cooking classes showcase New Zealand's array of seafood in a fun and social environment. The concept is based on 'Look, Cook, Eat': you start with a fun and entertaining one-hour cooking demonstration, go on to cook the recipes yourself with assistance from your chef and then enjoy a delicious seafood meal shared with friends – old and new.

New Zealand is blessed with many different species of fish but some stock levels are under more pressure than others. A strong concept behind the Seafood School philosophy is to introduce, test and taste species that you may not have tried before so that next time you have a recipe calling for a certain species, you can try something new. Give it a go and you may be pleasantly surprised.

A common misconception around seafood is that it is difficult to cook – often we stick with familiar recipes and flavours – but it is actually very quick to cook and goes so well with many different flavours. From simply pan-fried with olive oil, butter, lemon and fresh herbs to the flavours and spices of curries, from incredibly easy and impressive whole baked fish to the sweet, sour and salty combinations of Asian cuisines, it is time to move away from the tried and true and try something new.

Pop into your fish retailer every few days and ask them for the most cost-effective and fresh fish, then test different species with the same recipe to see what works for your palate. There is a wide range of New Zealand seafood that is incredibly cost-effective – you do not always need to go for the familiar choices. Use our species guide (page 20) to choose an option, or talk with your fish supplier, and test your choice in any of the recipes that call for 'market-fresh fish'.

Try to incorporate seafood in your weekly meals at least twice a week – the health benefits are proven (see page 10).

We are incredibly privileged to be able to catch our own seafood in New Zealand – whether through fishing, diving or snorkelling – and with continued informed management of the resource, we should be able to share the tradition with future generations.

Visit www.afm.co.nz for information on public cooking classes, corporate and team events and/or venue rental for special functions.

Jo Cooper
Manager, Auckland Seafood School

About this cookbook

The Complete New Zealand Seafood Cookbook is not just a compilation of inviting recipes; it is also a comprehensive seafood reference and a celebration of New Zealand's fishing industry. Our aim is to bring you fabulous recipes from our wonderful Seafood School regular chefs – John Campbell, Colin Doyle, Mark Dronjak, Marco Edwardes, Petra New and Steve Roberts – but also to create the 'go to' book for all that is New Zealand seafood. The collection of tried and true recipes showcases seafood in many different styles and flavours, from classic to unique. We hope to show you options with your species choices, introduce flavour combinations that you may not have previously tried and provide a range of recipes covering everything from everyday meals to special events.

If you have ever been given a whole fish by a sharing neighbour and pondered what to do with it, check out our species guide (page 20) to gauge the type of fish and best cooking techniques, and then work your way through the step-by-step filleting guide (page 14). Before you know it, you will have perfect (or near perfect) fillets ready for cooking.

Where does your fish come from?

Have you ever wondered how your fish gets from the ocean to your plate?

It is possible that your fish has come through an auction at the Auckland Fish Market. The auction sells well over 50 different species of fin-fish, shellfish and crustaceans. It is all very fresh as it has literally just come in off the boat.

At 6 a.m. every weekday registered buyers from all over New Zealand arrive at the Auckland Fish Market to purchase bins of fish in a Dutch-style auction (bidding starts high and then price lowers). Fishmongers, restaurateurs, supermarkets, fish and chip shop owners and agents purchasing on behalf of clients all head to this auction looking for the freshest and best-value seafood they can get their hands on.

The auction attracts supply from all over the country, from small owner–operators with one boat to fishing companies with large fishing fleets. The auction sells on behalf of the supplier and allows suppliers the ability to sell all their products in one location.

The most popular species are snapper, trevally, tarakihi and red gurnard. Most of these species are caught by trawlers, Danish seiners and long-liners operating on the east and west coasts of the North and South Island.

The auction also sells great volumes of grey mullet, flounder and kahawai, among others, that are caught in numerous harbours around the North Island by smaller operators using set and ring nets. This product is often caught the same day it is sold, so it is as fresh as it gets.

The Auckland Fish Market auction house is the home of all things seafood in Auckland and arguably New Zealand. A trip to watch the auction and get behind the scenes is an experience not to be missed.

Michael Sprague
Auction Manager, Auckland Fish Market

Fishing methods

Although there are many methods of catching fish, they fall into three main groups:
1. Catching fish singly or in schools using nets or spears.
2. Trapping fish in stationary gear, such as fish traps or set-nets.
3. Attracting fish to get caught on hooks using bait, artificial lures or other means, such as light.

The various fishing methods are:
- Netting: Typically a long, narrow and flat net, weighted at the bottom edge and supported at the top edge by floats.
- Lining methods: Most commonly used lining methods are hand-lines and long-lines. Long-lines consist of a main line running parallel to the bottom, with baited short lines (snoods) attached at intervals. The line is anchored at each end and held at the surface by floats.
- Trolling: Baited hooks or lures are towed behind a boat and fish are pulled aboard when caught. Designed for fast-moving surface fish.
- Trawling: The most important commercial fishing method in New Zealand, especially for deep-sea species. Trawling involves one or two fishing vessels towing a large net. Most New Zealand trawlers are single, rather than pair, trawlers. Nets are usually towed for two or three hours at a speed of three or four knots. Nets of both bottom and mid-water trawling are held open by two 'doors', which act as paravanes, or underwater kites.
- Danish seining: Used to encircle, herd and

finally trap the fish. A net bag, similar in shape to a trawl bag, is operated by a long, weighted rope fixed to each end. The two ropes are used to encircle the fish and also to haul the net in.
- Purse seining: Used to catch surface-dwelling species. Aerial spotter planes are usually used to locate the intended catch. The purse seine net is laid in a circle around the school. The net is then 'pursed', drawing the bottom closed and entrapping the fish. Purse seining cannot be used by recreational fishers.
- Beach seining/drag netting: Normally carried out using a length of net and an additional length of warp (rope). The net and warp are laid out from, and back to, the shore and retrieved by hauling on to the shore.
- Dredging: Used to gather scallops and oysters. To gather scallops, the fishing vessel tows a rigid steel-framed dredge along the sea floor. With oysters, a heavier ring mesh is typically used.
- Jigging: A method of catching squid by continuously lowering and retrieving lines from the fishing vessel. Jigging is generally done at night when squid are attracted by powerful lights on the vessel.
- Pots: Rock lobsters and blue cod are caught in pots, usually made of a steel frame covered with wire mesh. The pot is baited with fish and dropped from the boat on the end of a rope long enough to reach the bottom. The position of the pot is marked with floats so the pot can be easily recovered.
- Diving: Some commercial and recreational fishers dive for paua, scallops and rock lobsters. Paua may only be taken by divers using snorkels, not scuba gear.

Seafood industry information and sustainability

New Zealand is a world leader in fisheries management and supports an industry based on sustainable harvest and environmental principles.

Seafood New Zealand Limited works on

behalf of the New Zealand seafood industry. The industry is made up of approximately 2500 participating enterprises; including fishermen and aquaculturists, and family-owned, publicly listed and joint-venture seafood companies, fisheries management organisations and retailers.

By the early 1980s, fishing pressure had reduced the size of a number of New Zealand's major fisheries, particularly the inshore fisheries. Because of this, in 1986, New Zealand introduced the Quota Management System (QMS) with the aim of conserving major fisheries stocks and making the fishing industry more efficient.

The QMS requires the industry and government agencies to continually work together to assess stock levels of all quota-managed species. From these results, the Ministry for Primary Industries sets a yearly Total Allowable Commercial Catch (TACC) for each species.

Analysis and research shows that Alaska and New Zealand have led the world in management success by not waiting until drastic measures are needed to conserve, restore and rebuild marine resources. The research shows that New Zealand is an area where ecosystems have never been overfished and are effectively managed for ecological sustainability.

The Auckland Seafood School, as part of the Sanford Limited group, has adopted Sustainable Seafood as its motto and as an integrated and long-established seafood company it is devoted entirely to the responsible harvesting, farming, processing, storage and marketing of quality seafood and aquaculture products.

Please see www.sanford.co.nz and www.seafood.co.nz for more information on sustainability.

What is in seafood that makes it so good?

Fish is described as a 'body and brain stimulation protein', easily digested and rich in nutrients. These days there is great awareness of the incredible health benefits of regular fish meals and the recommendation is to include at least two fish meals per week in your diet in order to get the best omega-3 health benefits, since two high-quality types of omega-3 fatty acids are found only in seafood. Furthermore, seafood is:

- high in protein
- low in carbohydrates and saturated fats
- a good source of essential minerals and vitamins
- completely natural and easy to digest.

Fish is easily digested because it has a high proportion of muscle tissue protein and a low proportion of fat and connective tissue protein holding the muscle blocks together, and also because the muscle protein is made up of short-length fibres. Research shows that seafood has a unique combination of low total fat combined with a high percentage of good fats such as omega-3. This unique combination reduces the amount of blood cholesterol produced in the human body after eating a meal of fish.

Check out the Seafood New Zealand website for further information: www.seafood.co.nz/health.

Catching, handling, purchasing and storing fish

The catch

If you get the chance, take the opportunity to head out and catch your own fish. It truly is a great pleasure being out on the water – even if the fish are not biting you can enjoy relaxing in one of the beautiful bays, beaches and coves that New Zealand's coastline and its surrounding islands have to offer.

When fishing, take only what you need and be aware of the rules around recreational fishing in New Zealand waters. By acting responsibly we can all help to conserve the resource. Take a size-limit information booklet or sticker with you or download the New Zealand Fishing Rules app (at www.fish.govt.nz).

Handling undersize fish

Fish scales are covered with a mucous layer which helps prevent infections. Rough handling and dry hands can damage the mucous layer and reduce the chance of the fish surviving following release. To protect the scales, use wet cotton gloves, rubber gloves or a wet tea towel soaked in sea water to handle the fish while removing the hook. Extract the hook as carefully as possible. Try to push the hook back the way it came without tearing at the mouth. Get a secure grip with hook removers or long-nosed pliers. Do not squeeze the fish too hard as its internal organs are easily damaged, and gently slip the fish back into the water.

Killing your catch

'Ikijime' the fish immediately by inserting a spike directly into the brain. This kills the fish instantly and the blood contained in the fish flesh retracts, producing a better quality (and better tasting) fish fillet.

Have a fish slurry ready to maintain the quality of the fish by chilling immediately. A fish slurry that combines freshwater ice with seawater works well. Once chilled, store fish in a container and cover with ice.

There are no regulations that prohibit the filleting of fish at sea. However, if the fish in question is subject to a size limit it is advisable to only fillet larger fish where there is no doubt regarding the original fish size. You need to be able to satisfy any inspecting fishery officer as to whether the fillet came from a legal-sized fish.

Dispatching crayfish

Kill crayfish by either drowning in fresh water; holding down with a cloth and placing a large knife or spike through its head; or placing it in the freezer and letting it pass away in its sleep (take care not to freeze it solid).

Purchasing fish

Take time and care to understand the source of the fish you are purchasing. It is essential that sustainability of the resource is maintained. Ask your fishmonger where the fish was caught and landed. It is important to ensure that your fish supplier is part of the sustainable management system. We should all be aware of where seafood originates and that supplies of it are maintained under the QMS.

When purchasing seafood, keep an open mind about what you buy. Choose what looks best as well as what will suit the recipe you have in mind – or try something new!

A fresh fish smells of the sea and should not have a strong odour. It is firm to the touch rather than soft and mushy. The eyes should be bright, clear and shiny and the gills bright red. The scales (if any) should be intact and plentiful.

Storing fish

Always pack fish on ice once caught or purchased, as each hour the fish is at room temperature reduces its shelf life by a day. Ask your fishmonger to bag your purchase on ice. Store for up to five days in your fridge, ideally at 0°C. The freshness of the fish is of the utmost importance; therefore the period of storage should be kept to a minimum.

The best way to store fresh fish is to place the fish in a plastic bag or on a perforated tray. Place a layer of cling film over the fish and top with ice or a bag of ice. Store in a container that will hold the melted ice and replace the ice each day. Keep whole fish and fillets separate to avoid the risk of cross-contamination. Ensure the ice does not directly sit on the fish flesh.

Ideally, you shouldn't freeze fish as it has a short shelf-life (up to two months) and runs the risk of freezer burn if not stored properly. However, if you do have an excess supply, vacuum pack your fillets or wrap them tightly in cling film, date and name the pack and place in the freezer.

Storing shellfish

Live shellfish can be stored in your fridge for a day or ideally stored out of the fridge in a cool area under a cover of melting ice, ensuring the ice makes no direct contact with the shellfish. Place the shellfish in a self-draining vessel, e.g. a colander, and place in a sink or over a bowl. Lay a tea towel or cloth over the shellfish and top with the ice. Replenish the ice as required. Ideally purchase shellfish for use on the same day – they are usually readily available from your local supermarket, food store or fish market – and get them home and chilled as soon as possible.

To test if your shellfish are still alive prior to cooking, leave them at room temperature for 20 minutes and then tap the shells lightly until they close. If shell remains open the shellfish is dead – throw it away.

Preparing fish and shellfish

You will need a chopping board, a non-slip mat or wet tea towel (to place under the board to stop it from moving around) and a large sharp filleting knife.

Scaling

Using a de-scaler (or a butter knife or the side of a fork), hold the tail and, starting at the tail end, run the de-scaler along the skin to remove the scales. Be prepared for a mess – outside kitchens work well for this. If you are going to fillet and skin, don't worry about scaling the fish. The scales will be removed along with the skin.

Gutting

Insert the point of the knife into the vent and slice through to the head using the end third of the knife. Grab the intestines and remove. They tend to come out in one mass; however, you may require a small sharp knife to cut the attachment near the head end. Use a spoon to remove the blood line that runs along the spine inside the cavity. Rinse with cold water.

Filleting

Place the point of the knife under the fins at an angle, cutting towards the head through to the backbone. Hold the flap, lifting slightly and applying some pressure, and use the full length of the knife to run along the backbone – you will feel some friction, but keep moving the knife through in one continuous motion. Turn the fish over and repeat the same process. Be aware that the weight loss from filleting is approximately 40%, e.g. 1kg of whole fish equals about 600g of fresh fish fillets.

Boning and skinning

Remove the rib bones by sliding the knife along the length of the bones. Skin the fish by holding the tail end of the fillet and angling down into the skin, using the whole knife in a continuous movement. Once skinned, locate the bones that run through the middle of the fillet by running your finger along the line and then remove by cutting out in a 'V' shape.

Pin-boning and skinning salmon

You will need pin-boning tweezers, a small bowl of cold water to rinse tweezers, a chopping board, non-slip mat or wet tea towel (to place under the board to stop it from moving around) and a large sharp knife.

1. Leave the skin on while pin-boning. Place the fillet on the board and run the back of the knife along the line of the bones to raise them out of the flesh.

2. Use the tweezers to start extracting the bones. Take up the pressure of the bone (make sure you have a good grip) and pull out in the direction the bone is lying. Do not wriggle the bone as you will break up the flesh. Keep your hands free of the flesh as much as possible to reduce the chance of damage. Rinse the tweezers and bones out in the bowl of water as you go.

3. Rub your thumb gently along the line to ensure there are no bones left – the bones run two-thirds of the way along the fillet

from the head end. The small bones at the head end can be tricky. If you are having trouble removing these then cut the end off.
4. It is easier to skin a whole fillet than a smaller portion of salmon as you have better grip to hold the skin. Start at the tail end and make a small incision 5mm into the flesh. Hold the skin at the end of the fillet and angle your knife into the skin. For oily fish you can dip your hands into salt for a better grip. Work your way along the fillet in one smooth motion (to achieve the best result, don't stop), cutting 30 per cent and pulling the skin 70 per cent.

Filleting flat fish
Starting at the head, run the tip of the knife around the edges of the fish. A less rigid filleting knife is suitable for this. Run the knife along the bone line through to the other side. Trim the edges of the fillet to tidy it up.

Cleaning mussels
1. Scrub each mussel shell with a stiff brush to remove grit and weed. Use a small knife to carefully remove barnacles if required, taking care not to damage the shell.
2. Use your fingers to grip and remove the hairy beards (byssal threads) that protrude from the inside of the mussel (yank quickly toward the hinge end to ensure you do not damage the mussel meat). Any difficult to remove bits can be discarded once the mussel is steamed open.
3. Check the cooked mussel meat for small crabs and any excess threads and remove foot if desired.

Purging sand from shellfish
Option 1: Place shellfish in a bucket of seawater and add a handful of oats. Leave overnight in a cool place. The shellfish will feed on the oats and purge themselves of sand in the process. Option 2: Place a cake rack in the bottom of a container and place the shellfish on top of the rack. Fill the bucket with cold water and leave for a couple of hours. Gently remove the shellfish and tip out the water. If there is sand in the bottom of the bucket, repeat the process until the water runs clear.

Shucking oysters
If you are opening large quantities of oysters, invest in an oyster shucker; they are specifically designed to protect and guard your hands when opening the shell. A short thin-edged knife will also work. Wrap the oyster in a tea towel with the flatter side facing up and work the shucker or knife into the shell near the hinge, then move it gently towards the hinge and twist to break the shell open. Remove the top shell and gently release the oyster.

Seafood cooking techniques
There are various techniques involved in cooking seafood, the most popular of which are pan-frying, barbecuing, steaming, poaching and baking. Details of how to carry out each of these cooking techniques are outlined below. Whichever technique you are using, to test for doneness press the flesh of the fish prior to cooking to gauge its texture. The fish is cooked when the flesh is more firm to the touch and the flesh flakes easily.

How to pan-fry fish fillets
You will need:
2 fish fillets, skin on, scaled and boned
Salt and freshly ground pepper
2 tbsp grapeseed or canola oil
15g butter

1. Remove fish fillets from the fridge 15 minutes prior to cooking. Choose a frying pan large enough to accommodate the fillets.
2. Season fish fillets.
3. Heat the pan until hot, then add the oil. Place fish fillets into the hot pan skin-side down. Cook until the edges of the fish start turning white. Cooking time will depend on the thickness of the fish; however, when you notice a good line of white showing along the edges carefully turn fillets with a fish slice.
4. Add butter to the pan. It should create a froth that you can spoon over the skin of the fish fillets. Do not add the butter at the beginning of cooking as it will burn – by adding near the end of cooking, the butter will give the fish a glossy shine and light buttery flavour.
5. Turn the heat off. The fish will continue to cook through from the heat of the pan. Once again, cooking time will depend on the thickness of the fillet.

How to barbecue fish fillets
You will need:
2 fish fillets, skin on, scaled and boned
Salt and freshly ground pepper
3 tbsp grapeseed or canola oil
1 lemon, cut in half

1. Remove fish fillets from the fridge 15 minutes prior to cooking.
2. Heat the barbecue hot plate until hot (use a barbecue mat if preferred).
3. Season fish fillets with salt and pepper and drizzle with oil.

4. Place fish fillets onto the hot plate skin-side down. Cook until the edges of the fish start turning white. Cooking time will depend on the thickness of the fish; however, when you notice a good line of white showing along the edges carefully turn the fillets with a fish slice.
5. Cook for a further 2–3 minutes, then squeeze lemon juice over the fish fillets just before removing them from the barbecue.

How to steam a whole fish
You will need:
1 whole fish, scaled and gutted
Salt and freshly ground pepper
1 lemon, cut into slices
1 bunch coriander, roughly chopped
1 banana leaf (available at Asian supermarkets and specialty foodstores)

1. Make incisions into the flesh on both sides until you hit the bone. Season with salt and pepper, then line the fish cavity with lemon slices and coriander.
2. Prepare the base of the steamer (we have used a wok base) by placing approximately 1½ cups water into the wok (this will depend on the size of the wok/pot you are using) and heating it to create steam. Line the steamer with banana leaf. Place the fish on top of the banana leaf, cover with steamer lid and place into the wok base.
3. Steam for approximately 12–15 minutes, depending on the size of the fish. Do not be put off by the eyes – they are a delicacy to some!

Scallop and goat's cheese fritters

SERVES 4 | Recipe by Mark Dronjak

Sliced scallops and grated courgette add the texture; the lemon and goat's cheese add the bite!

2 medium–large eggs, beaten
1 tbsp baking powder
100–140g plain flour
100–150ml full-fat milk
Sea salt and freshly ground pepper
180g fresh scallops, sliced, including roe
2 courgettes, grated
85g goat's cheese, cut into small dice or crumbled
Zest of ½ lemon
Olive oil
1 lemon, cut into wedges
Sprigs of flat-leaf parsley, for garnish

1. In a bowl combine beaten eggs, baking powder, a little flour and a little milk. Slowly add more flour and milk as required to make a thick batter. Season to taste.

2. Add scallops, courgette, goat's cheese and lemon zest to the batter mix and fold in carefully. Particular care should be taken not to break up the ingredients when mixing. Adjust seasoning.

3. Heat a large pan and add a little olive oil. Add mix in small bite-sized portions. Cook fritters, turning once; do not overcook or the fritters can become tough.

4. Serve fritters with lemon wedges and parsley.

Black pepper market fish salad

SERVES 4 | Recipe by Petra New

The heat of the black pepper works well with the refreshing mint and lime.

2 cups mesclun leaves
2 tbsp chopped fresh mint leaves
1 tbsp chopped fresh coriander
Juice of 2 limes
1 tbsp crushed palm sugar
1 tbsp fish sauce
1 heaped tbsp freshly ground pepper
¼ cup rice flour
400g market-fresh fish fillets, skinned, boned, cubed
Canola oil
1 spring onion, sliced
2 cloves garlic, sliced
½ long red chilli, deseeded and sliced
1 heaped tbsp chopped fresh coriander

1. In a bowl, mix together mesclun with mint and coriander.

2. In a jug mix lime juice, palm sugar and fish sauce until the palm sugar has dissolved.

3. Mix together pepper and rice flour and toss fish in mix to coat.

4. Heat canola oil in a pan and fry fish for a few minutes until crispy and golden all over. Drain on paper towels.

5. Stir-fry spring onion, garlic and chilli until golden. Remove from the pan and lightly toss with chopped coriander and fish, taking care not to break up the fish.

6. Dress salad and arrange on four separate plates, with fish on top.

Poached seafood roulade, spinach and sauce vierge

SERVES 4 AS A MAIN OR 6 AS A STARTER | Recipe by Marco Edwardes

Perfect for a special occasion dinner at home.

FISH FARCE
200g fresh white fish
Sea salt and freshly ground pepper
Juice of 1 lemon
1 egg white
60–70ml cold cream

SAUCE VIERGE
1 cup olive oil
3 tomatoes, peeled, deseeded and
    finely diced
Juice of 1 lemon
2 tbsp finely chopped basil leaves
1 tbsp finely chopped chervil leaves
1 clove garlic, minced
6 coriander seeds, crushed
Sea salt and freshly ground pepper

200–300g fresh salmon
Sea salt and freshly ground pepper
300g baby spinach, washed
20g butter
1 onion, finely sliced
1 clove garlic, crushed
Pinch of sugar for spinach

1. To prepare fish farce (stuffing), cut fish into small cubes and place in a stainless steel bowl. Season. Drizzle with lemon juice and add egg white. Mix well and place in freezer for 10–15 minutes.

2. Remove fish mix from freezer and place in a food processor. Using the pulse button, pulse fish into a fine paste. Slowly add cream to the fish mix until well combined. Season to taste.

3. Pass mix through a fine sieve (to remove any bones or scales). Place fish farce in a bowl, cover and place in fridge until needed.

4. To make sauce vierge, combine all ingredients in a bowl, mix gently and season to taste. Set aside until required.

5. To make the roulade, spread a sheet of cling film on the kitchen bench. Slice salmon very thinly. Place salmon slices on cling film, slightly overlapping. Season to taste.

6. Spread fish farce onto salmon. Cover with a few of the spinach leaves.

7. Roll up the roulade on the long side, making sure it is not too tight and that the cling film is not rolled inside the roulade. Roll again in a sheet of tin foil, closing the ends tightly.

8. Poach the roulade in a pot of simmering water (do not boil) for 8–10 minutes. Remove from water and place on a plate. Remove the wrapping and cut into 4 or 6 pieces.

9. Heat butter in a medium-sized pan. Sauté onion and garlic, then add the rest of the baby spinach and cook until wilted. Season to taste, adding sugar if desired.

10. Serve sliced roulade on wilted spinach with sauce vierge that has been slightly warmed.

Flounder paupiettes with prawns, spinach and lemon beurre blanc

SERVES 4 | Recipe by Marco Edwardes

An elegant French classic. Bon appétit!

600g flounder fillets (or similar flat fish
   such as sole or brill)
Sea salt and freshly ground pepper
100g cold smoked salmon slices
12 prawn cutlets
100ml fish stock (see recipe page 272)
100g jasmine rice
300ml vegetable stock

LEMON BEURRE BLANC
1 clove garlic, crushed
1 shallot, finely diced
Zest and juice of 1 lemon
250ml white wine
5 tbsp cold unsalted butter
Salt and freshly ground pepper
Small bunch fresh dill, chopped

15g butter
1 shallot, finely sliced
1 clove garlic, crushed
600g baby spinach, washed
Salt and freshly ground pepper

1. Preheat oven to 180°C.

2. Place fish fillets on a work surface and season to taste. Arrange some smoked salmon on top of each fillet followed by a couple of prawns. Roll up each fillet to enclose its contents.

3. Butter an ovenproof dish and place paupiettes side by side in the dish. Pour fish stock over them and cover with tin foil. Bake for 7–10 minutes.

4. In the meantime, place rice in a small pot and add vegetable stock. Bring to the boil, cover with a lid and simmer at low heat until water is absorbed and rice is cooked.

5. While rice is cooking, to make the lemon beurre blanc, heat another small pot and sauté garlic and shallot. Add lemon zest and juice and white wine and reduce liquid by half.

6. Remove pan from the heat and whisk in butter a little at a time until sauce is smooth and shiny. Adjust seasoning and pass sauce through a fine sieve. Keep warm.

7. In a large saucepan, heat butter, shallot and garlic. Cook until shallot is translucent. Add spinach and wilt. Season to taste.

8. Stir dill through beurre blanc.

9. To serve, place wilted spinach on warm dinner plates, top with paupiettes and spoon over beurre blanc. Serve with rice on the side.

Prawn and chorizo skewers with beetroot and feta salad

SERVES 4 | Recipe by John Campbell

Make sure you use good-quality chorizo on the skewers for premium flavour.

24 small baby beetroot, trimmed and
    washed but not peeled, cut in half

Sea salt

90g pecans

320g chorizo

16 raw prawn cutlets

2 tsp paprika

2 tsp cumin

80ml extra virgin olive oil

Salt and freshly ground pepper

1½ tbsp verjuice

1 tsp wholegrain mustard

1 tsp honey

150g rocket

100g firm feta, sliced

1. Place 8 wooden skewers in water to soak. Preheat oven to 200°C.

2. Sprinkle beetroot with sea salt and roast for approximately 20 minutes. In a separate dish, dry-roast pecans for 15 minutes.

3. Cut chorizo into 16 pieces. Marinate prawns and chorizo with spices and a little olive oil for 10 minutes, or longer if you have time.

4. Thread 2 prawns and 2 pieces of chorizo onto each skewer. Brush with a little olive oil and barbecue for 2 minutes on each side. If desired, barbecue beetroot for a bit of colour. Season both items.

5. To make dressing, combine verjuice, mustard and honey in a jar and shake well. Mix rocket with dressing, pecans and beetroot. Place feta on top (don't mix or you'll get beetroot juice running through). Season to taste.

6. Serve salad in bowls and place two skewers each on top.

Herb-crusted fish fillets with bean and potato salad and salsa verde

SERVES 4 | Recipe by Mark Dronjak

A great-looking dish full of flavour and Mediterranean influences.

SALSA VERDE

1–2 cloves garlic
¼ cup capers
4 anchovy fillets
2 cups finely chopped flat-leaf parsley
Juice of 1 lemon
80–120ml extra virgin olive oil
Sea salt and freshly ground pepper
4–6 tbsp red wine vinegar

2½ cups of herbs (e.g. flat-leaf parsley, coriander, watercress)
Olive oil
Sea salt and freshly ground black pepper
400g market-fresh seasonal fish fillets (e.g. monkfish, ling, lemonfish or hapuku)
250g potatoes, peeled and diced
250g fresh green beans
1 small radicchio lettuce, leaves torn
Juice of 1 lemon

1. To make salsa verde, finely chop garlic, capers and anchovies and add parsley. Combine mixture in a bowl and squeeze over lemon juice; add a good lug of quality olive oil. Season to taste, then add vinegar.

2. Roughly chop herbs for the crust, add a good drizzle of olive oil and season well.

3. Rub herb crust onto one side of each fillet. Set aside until ready to cook.

4. Blanch potatoes until firm. Blanch beans whole, then refresh under cold water and drain well. Combine potatoes and green beans and torn radicchio leaves. Dress with a little olive oil and lemon juice and season. Toss.

5. Place fish fillets on the barbecue grill and sear for a few minutes on both sides.

6. Serve with salad and dress with salsa verde.

Whitebait flan

SERVES 4 | Recipe by John Campbell

Take care not to let this pastry brown too much. You can vary the flan by adding salmon pieces and blanched spinach leaves, or serve it with other sauces, such as Hollandaise (see recipe page 265) or meunière, or herb butters (see recipes page 270).

PASTRY

⅓ cup milk

2 tsp yeast granules

Few pinches of sugar

2½ cups plain flour

150g butter, softened

2 egg yolks

Salt

¼ cup white wine vinegar

WHITEBAIT FILLING

2 eggs

⅓ cup cream

⅓ cup milk

300g whitebait

Salt and freshly ground pepper

Lime (or lemon) glaze (see recipe page 264)

1. To make pastry, warm milk in a pan over a low heat on the stovetop and add yeast. Sprinkle a few grains of sugar over yeast (this makes the mixture work faster). Leave for 15 minutes in a warm place.

2. Put flour in a large bowl, make a well in the centre and add milk and yeast mixture. Leave for 10 minutes.

3. Add butter, egg yolks and salt to taste and mix well. Rest mixture for 15 minutes before using.

4. Preheat oven to 150°C.

5. Roll out pastry and line four 11cm flan rings. Brush each with vinegar and fill with baking paper and dry beans. Bake without colouring for about 8 minutes.

6. To make whitebait filling, beat eggs in a bowl and add cream and milk. Mix in whitebait and seasoning to taste.

7. Brush each cooked pastry flan with a little more vinegar, then fill with whitebait filling. Bake for about 15 minutes without colouring. Remove from oven.

8. Serve immediately drizzled with lime glaze.

Warm squid salad with summer leaves and croutons

SERVES 4 | Recipe by John Campbell

Use any seasonal salad greens to create a light and tasty summer salad to enjoy around the barbecue with friends.

CROUTONS

½ day-old baguette or Turkish pide, sliced

1 tbsp olive oil

Sea salt and freshly ground pepper

300–400g Agria potatoes

2 pinches saffron

50ml olive oil

2 tsp chopped rosemary leaves

2 cloves garlic, sliced

Salt and freshly ground pepper

200g courgettes, sliced into strips

200g arrow squid, cleaned and sliced

50g spinach leaves

50g rocket

50g watercress

50g red chard

1½ tbsp vincotto (see glossary page 276)

2 tbsp olive oil

1. Preheat oven to 185°C.

2. To make croutons, drizzle bread with olive oil and season. Place on an oiled baking tray and bake for 7 minutes.

3. Slice potatoes into wedges. Blanch in boiling water with saffron for 5 minutes. Drain and cool.

4 Place a liner on the barbecue plate. Put a little oil on the liner and cook saffron potatoes with rosemary and garlic until crisp. Season to taste.

5. Toss courgette strips in some more oil and cook on the grill plate until lightly coloured.

6. Dry squid, mix with remaining oil and place on the hot grill plate until cooked.

7. In a large bowl, mix salad leaves with cooked potato, squid and courgette. Drizzle with vincotto, croutons and oil. Season to taste.

8. Serve on a large platter.

DID YOU KNOW?

New Zealand arrow squid are two of over 80 squid species found in New Zealand waters. Their relative the giant squid, at around 12 metres from tail to tentacle tip, is 12 times their length.

Sushi and sashimi

MAKES 4 LARGE OR 6 SMALL ROLLS OF SUSHI OR A PLATTER OF SASHIMI | Recipe by Steve Roberts

The trick to perfect sushi and sashimi is perfectly cooked rice and the freshest fish available.

SUSHI RICE
(MAKES 6 CUPS COOKED RICE)
3 cups short-grain rice
3 cups water
3 tsp sake
5 tbsp rice vinegar
2 tbsp sugar

4–6 sheets toasted nori (seaweed)
200g selection of freshly caught raw fish
  (salmon, tuna, salmon roe, etc.),
  thinly sliced
1 egg omelette, cooked and thinly sliced
½ cucumber, julienned
½ avocado, thinly sliced
½ red or green capsicum, julienned
3 tbsp soy sauce, to serve
20g pickled ginger, to serve
30g prepared wasabi (or use powder and
  add water according to instructions),
  to serve

1. To make sushi rice, wash rice in cold water, then drain. Place rice and water in a pot with a fitted lid and bring to the boil. Stir once, then reduce heat and simmer for 10 minutes, ensuring the lid is not lifted. Turn off heat and leave with lid on for a further 10 minutes. Alternatively, use a rice cooker.

2. Turn rice out onto a large flat surface.

3. Mix together sake, rice vinegar and sugar. Fold vinegar mix through rice, taking care not to squash rice grains, and leave to cool.

4. To make sushi rolls, lay a sheet of nori on a bamboo sushi mat. Using clean, wet hands to stop rice from sticking, spread enough rice over nori to cover it, leaving 2cm of nori at the top and bottom. Place selected fillings in a centred horizontal strip on top of rice.

5. To roll the sushi, hook your thumbs under the end of the mat that is closest to you. Hold filling in place with your fingers while lifting the edge of the mat away from you, towards the farthest side. Roll the mat in one stroke to create your sushi roll.

6. Using a clean, wet, sharp knife cut sushi roll into individual pieces about 2cm in width. Clean knife after each slice. Repeat for each sheet of nori, varying filling combinations.

7. Alternatively, in clean, wet hands roll a small amount of rice to create a rectangular shape. Spread a small amount of wasabi across rice and top with thinly sliced fish. Garnish with salmon roe.

8. To make sashimi, thinly slice your choice of fresh raw fish and arrange on a platter.

9. Serve your sushi and sashimi with soy sauce, pickled ginger and wasabi.

Barbecued tandoori prawn and pineapple skewers with minted yoghurt

SERVES 4 | Recipe by Petra New

Tandoori on the barbecue gives prawns a more authentic flavour.

TANDOORI PASTE

1 tsp coriander seeds

1 tsp cumin seeds

½ tsp chilli powder

2cm fresh ginger, chopped

½ tsp salt

Juice of 1 lemon

1 tbsp tomato purée

½ cup plain unsweetened yoghurt

24 raw shelled prawns

½ pineapple, peeled and cubed (same size as prawns for even cooking)

MINTED YOGHURT DIPPING SAUCE

¼ cup fresh mint leaves

½ cup plain unsweetened yoghurt

1 tsp liquid honey

1. Place 8 bamboo skewers in water to soak.

2. To make tandoori paste, dry-roast coriander and cumin seeds in a pan. When fragrant, remove from heat and add chilli powder. Grind using a mortar and pestle and add ginger, salt and lemon juice. Transfer to a bowl and add the tomato purée and yoghurt.

3. Gently stir prawns through the tandoori paste and leave to marinate for at least 10 minutes.

4. To make minted yoghurt dipping sauce, combine mint, yoghurt and honey in a jug and blend.

5. Thread a prawn onto a skewer and then a pineapple cube, and repeat until you have 3 prawns and 3 pineapple cubes. Repeat to use all the prawns and pineapple.

6. Chargrill skewers on the barbecue over medium–high heat until cooked, approximately 2–3 minutes on each side.

7. Serve skewers with minted yoghurt dipping sauce.

Whitebait fritters

SERVES 4 | Recipe by John Campbell

This makes a great treat for Sunday breakfast.

4 eggs
300g whitebait
White pepper
75g butter
2 lemons, cut into wedges, to serve

1. Beat eggs in a bowl until well combined and add whitebait and white pepper to taste. Mix well.

2. Heat a non-stick omelette pan over a medium heat and add a little of the butter. When butter is hot, add 3 tablespoons of whitebait mixture.

3. Cook fritter for a couple of minutes, then turn over and cook the other side. Remove from pan and keep warm. Repeat until you have cooked the required number of fritters.

4. Serve at once with lemon wedges and hot buttered toast.

COOK'S NOTE
A simple way to cook whitebait is to dust the whitebait in flour before frying them in hot oil (remember to turn them often).

Mussel fritters ▶

SERVES 4 | Recipe by John Campbell

A simple, textured fritter that looks good and tastes even better.

500g mussels, cleaned
½ carrot, grated
1 courgette, grated
1 onion or spring onion, finely diced
⅓ cup rice flour
3 eggs
1 tbsp chopped flat-leaf parsley
Salt and freshly ground pepper
50ml oil
1 lemon, cut into wedges, to serve

1. Place 200ml water in a large lidded pot and bring to the boil. Add mussels and cook, covered, for approximately 4 minutes, until open. Cool and shell mussels.

2. Remove and discard the tongue and beard from the cooked mussels. Chop mussels finely or give them a quick whiz in the food processor (not for too long).

3. Add remaining ingredients (except oil and lemon wedges) and mix well.

4. Heat oil in a shallow frying pan. When hot, drop in spoonfuls of batter. Cook on each side for 3–4 minutes.

5. Repeat until all the batter is used.

6. Serve with dressed rocket leaves and your favourite pesto or chutney with lemon wedges on the side.

Grilled Caesar salad with barbecued scallops and prawns

SERVES 4 | Recipe by Marco Edwardes

A little twist – grilled lettuce! – on an old favourite.

ANCHOVY DRESSING

2 anchovy fillets, drained and chopped

1 clove garlic, chopped

½ cup olive oil

¼ tsp salt

¼ tsp freshly ground pepper

1 egg

2 tbsp fresh lemon juice (or to taste)

8 × 5mm-thick baguette slices

3 baby lettuces (romaine, cos or gem)

200g scallops

200g raw prawn cutlets

Olive oil

Salt and freshly ground pepper

80g Parmesan, shaved

4 roma tomatoes, washed and quartered

1 lemon, cut into wedges or thick slices

1. To make anchovy dressing, purée anchovies, garlic, olive oil, salt and pepper in a blender until smooth. Add egg and lemon juice. Blend for 1–2 minutes until emulsified, and adjust seasoning to taste.

2. Prepare grill or barbecue to a medium–hot heat. Brush both sides of baguette slices with some anchovy dressing, reserving some for later. Grill bread on the barbecue, turning occasionally until toasted, for 1–2 minutes.

3. Discard outer leaves from lettuces and cut lettuce hearts in half lengthwise. Grill on barbecue until grill marks start to appear (approximately 2 minutes). Cut lettuce crosswise into 5cm-wide strips and transfer to a bowl.

4. Place washed and dried scallops and prawns in a bowl. Season to taste and coat with a little olive oil. Barbecue scallops and prawns on the hot plate for 1 minute or until just cooked.

5. Halve or quarter toast slices and add to lettuce along with Parmesan. Toss the salad with just enough dressing to coat.

6. To serve, place dressed salad on plates, arrange quartered tomatoes around and place seafood on top. Serve lemon on the side.

Fishcakes topped with eggplant dip

SERVES 4 | Recipe by John Campbell

Enjoy any leftover dip served with breads and hummus.

EGGPLANT DIP

1 eggplant

1½ tbsp olive oil

2 cloves garlic, crushed

1 tbsp chopped fresh coriander

½ tsp ground cumin

Pinch of cayenne pepper

Juice of 1 lemon

Sea salt

200g soft white fish (e.g. snapper, tarakihi or gurnard)

50ml olive oil

200g Agria potatoes, cooked and grated

1 fresh chilli, deseeded (optional) and chopped, or ½ tsp dried chilli

2 cloves garlic, chopped

1 tbsp capers, chopped

Zest of 1 lemon

1 tbsp each chopped fresh parsley and coriander

Salt

Plain flour, to dust

Juice of 1 lemon

Olive oil for serving

1. Preheat oven to 210°C.

2. To make eggplant dip, cut eggplant in half lengthwise and brush with oil. Bake the two halves for about 30 minutes or until soft.

3. When cool enough to handle, scoop out flesh and mash with a fork. Add remaining ingredients and season to taste.

4. Pan-fry fish in a hot pan with some of the oil. Allow to cool.

5. Break fish into small pieces and mix with potato, chilli, garlic, capers, lemon zest, herbs and salt.

6. Using a ladle or small measuring cup, portion into equal sizes. Dust fishcakes with flour, shape and pan-fry for a few minutes on each side in remaining oil.

7. Serve with a squeeze of lemon juice, a sprinkle of olive oil and topped with a quenelle of the eggplant dip.

Wok-fried black bean pipi

SERVES 4 | Recipe by Steve Roberts

Black beans and pipi work so well together and this dish is quick and easy.

800g pipi, purged
1 tbsp light olive oil
1–2 tbsp sesame oil
1 tbsp salted fermented black beans, chopped
2 cloves garlic, finely chopped
3cm piece of ginger, peeled and finely chopped
1 large red chilli, deseeded and finely sliced
4 tbsp Chinese rice wine (Shaoxing)
1 tbsp dark soy sauce
Caster sugar to taste
1 spring onion, sliced

1. Heat both oils in a lidded wok. Add black beans, garlic, ginger and chilli. Stir-fry for 20–30 seconds.

2. Add pipi to the wok and stir-fry for 1 minute. Add rice wine and soy sauce. Cover with lid until pipis open. Add sugar to taste. To serve, garnish with spring onion and serve with steamed rice.

Tataki of tuna ▶

SERVES 4 | Recipe by Steve Roberts

This dish is light yet full of flavour.

400g sushi-grade tuna loin
2 tbsp freshly ground pepper
2 tbsp olive oil

PONZU VINAIGRETTE
250ml lemon juice
500ml rice wine vinegar
375ml soy sauce
125ml mirin
Zest of 1 lemon

125g micro greens
¼ carrot, julienned
Olive oil for drizzling
1 tbsp chopped chives
1 tbsp toasted sesame seeds (optional)
10 cherry tomatoes, quartered

1. Cut tuna loin into a long triangle shape and dredge it with black pepper.

2. Heat olive oil in a sauté pan over a medium–high heat. Add the tuna and sear for about 10 seconds on each side. Transfer tuna to a tray and refrigerate for half and hour.

3. To make ponzu vinaigrette, combine ingredients in a non-reactive saucepan and bring to the boil. Set aside to cool.

4. Slice tuna into 5mm slices and arrange on a serving plate. Dress micro greens and carrot with a little oil and arrange over tuna. Drizzle with vinaigrette and garnish with chives, sesame seeds (if using) and cherry tomatoes.

Sea cucumber with sorbet

MAKES APPROXIMATELY 20 | Recipe by Jason McGeorge

Not everyone's seafood pick, but try this recipe – you might be pleasantly surprised! Begin preparation a day before you wish to serve it.

2 sea cucumbers
1 red capsicum, deseeded and finely diced
1 yellow capsicum, deseeded and finely diced
2 medium red onions, finely diced
2–3 tomatoes, peeled and roughly diced
1 tsp lemon juice
Salt and freshly ground pepper
300ml coconut milk (not too thick)
100g lemon, lime and cucumber sorbet
    (or similar citrus sorbet – available from all
    good supermarkets)

1. Clean sea cucumbers by scrubbing outer skin to remove any loose matter. Slice in half lengthwise and scrape out innards, including membrane lines. Soak in salted water for 24 hours.

2. Remove sea cucumber halves from salted water and pat dry on paper towels. Briefly blanch sea cucumbers until just firm; refresh in iced water.

3. Cut sea cucumber into thin slices and combine with capsicum, onion, tomato, lemon juice, seasoning and coconut milk. Allow to marinate overnight. Season again to taste.

4. Serve in Asian spoons with a 5g scoop of sorbet.

Whelks in vinaigrette

SERVES 4 | Recipe by Jason McGeorge

The peppery horopito and manuka honey in this recipe create a delicious flavour pairing with the texture of the whelks.

VINAIGRETTE
20ml fresh lemon juice
65ml horopito avocado oil
2 tsp Dijon mustard
½ tsp manuka honey
1 clove garlic, crushed
Salt and freshly ground pepper

1kg whelks

1. To make vinaigrette, combine all ingredients and mix to create a light emulsion.

2. In a pot of boiling water, blanch whelks in their shells for 2 minutes, then refresh in iced water.

3. Remove whelk meat with a hook. Pat dry and slice very thinly.

4. Combine with vinaigrette to serve.

COOK'S NOTE
The edible part of the whelk is the muscle (also known as the foot) and it is best to remove the digestive gland, as it may contain toxins.

White fish with chilli, Mexican herbs and green olives

SERVES 4 | Recipe by Colin Doyle

This is based on a dish that originated in the port city of Veracruz, where Spanish ships laden with spices from the Old World landed in the New World. Think of it as what 'fusion cuisine' may have tasted like hundreds of years ago.

4 × 180g portions firm white fish (e.g. ling, hapuku, monkfish)

Juice of 1 lime

Sea salt

4 large tomatoes or 1½ × 400g cans whole tomatoes

Olive oil

1 large onion, thinly sliced

2 cloves garlic, finely chopped

2 tbsp capers

15 large green olives, pitted and roughly chopped

2 whole pickled jalapeño chillies and 2 tbsp jalapeño pickling liquid

1 bay leaf

5cm stick cinnamon

2 whole cloves

250ml fish stock (see recipe page 272)

¼ tsp dried oregano

1 sprig thyme

2 sprigs flat-leaf parsley, finely chopped, for garnish

1. Place fish in a non-reactive bowl and sprinkle with lime juice and salt. Set aside for a few minutes to marinate (up to 1 hour) while the sauce is prepared.

2. Quarter tomatoes and deseed. Reserve seeds and juice. Roughly chop tomatoes. Strain juice from seeds and add to chopped tomatoes (if using canned tomatoes you don't need to remove the seeds).

3. Heat a large sauté pan over a medium heat. Warm some olive oil and gently fry onion until golden brown.

4. Add garlic to onion. Fry for a minute or so and then add tomatoes. Allow to simmer for a couple of minutes to reduce some of the tomato juice.

5. Rinse capers and mix together with olives. Add half to the sauce and reserve the remainder for garnish.

6. Halve jalapeños lengthwise and remove stem and seeds. Slice into strips. Add to sauce along with reserved pickling liquid.

7. Add bay leaf, cinnamon, whole cloves, fish stock, oregano and thyme. Cook sauce for 5 minutes, then add marinated fish to poach in the sauce. Season to taste.

8. Serve fish garnished with reserved capers, olives and parsley.

Salad of fennel-crusted kingfish with orange, watercress, fennel and olives

SERVES 4 | Recipe by Marco Edwardes

Perfect for a summer lunch with family and friends. This recipe also works well with tuna or mahi-mahi.

FENNEL SPICE MIX

100g fennel seeds
2 tbsp black peppercorns
1 tbsp sea salt

4 × 80g kingfish fillets, skinned and boned
Cooking oil

SALAD

200g fennel bulbs, finely sliced
3 oranges, peeled and segmented
80g black Kalamata olives, pitted
Handful of fresh watercress
10 fresh mint leaves
1 long red chilli, deseeded and finely sliced
50ml olive oil
Sea salt and black pepper

1. To prepare fennel spice mix, combine ingredients in a pan over medium heat and cook until the spices are fragrant. Allow to cool, then grind with a mortar and pestle or spice grinder.

2. Roll kingfish fillets in 2 tablespoons of spice mix.

3. Heat barbecue. Place a liner on the barbecue plate. Brush with oil and cook kingfish for 30–40 seconds on each side until fish is sealed evenly but still rare in the centre. Set aside and keep warm.

4. Place all salad ingredients in a bowl and mix together well.

5. To serve, divide salad among 4 plates. Cut kingfish into 5mm slices and arrange on salad.

Coconut and chilli seafood parcels

SERVES 4 | Recipe by Petra New

This easy yet delicious marinade serves all seafood well. Let your imagination go wild – a combination parcel always feels a little indulgent.

2 cloves garlic, crushed

1cm fresh ginger, grated

2 tbsp sweet chilli sauce

400ml can coconut cream

1 tbsp fish sauce

Juice of 1 lime

¼ cup chopped fresh coriander

Cooking spray

2 squid tubes, sliced

4 × 100g fish fillets, boned, skin on

12 large mussels, cleaned

8 pipi, purged

12 scallops

¼ red onion, sliced

4 cups steamed jasmine rice, to serve

1. In a jug mix together garlic, ginger, sweet chilli sauce, coconut cream, fish sauce, lime juice and coriander.

2. Lay out 4 large pieces of tin foil (big enough to hold all seafood) and top each with a piece of baking paper slightly smaller than the foil. Spray with non-stick spray.

3. Arrange squid on the paper, then top with fish. Top this with remaining seafood. Sprinkle the sliced red onion over seafood, then pour over coconut cream mix.

4. Bring together two sides of the foil and fold. Repeat, making a double fold, then fold over the other ends twice as well. This makes sure neither the steam nor the cooking juices escape.

5. Place parcels on the flat plate of a barbecue on medium–high heat and cook with hood down for 4–6 minutes.

6. To serve, break open the middle of each parcel, pushing the sides away to expose the seafood. Serve with rice.

Paddle crabs

SERVES 4 | Recipe by John Campbell

This is a delicious way of cooking whole crabs. Try making this on a barbecue, but use oil instead of butter, and don't have the heat too high. Chargrill the pieces of crab and add the chopped garlic and spring onions just before serving.

4 paddle crabs, about 400g each
   (alive if possible)

2 carrots

2 onions

2 stalks celery

1 bouquet garni

100g butter

4 cloves garlic, chopped

½ cup dry white wine

2 tsp chopped fresh ginger (optional)

Freshly ground pepper

2 spring onions, chopped

1. Place crabs in the freezer for 10–15 minutes to stun them.

2. Bring a large pot of water to the boil and add carrot, onion, celery and bouquet garni. Add crabs to the pot and bring the liquid back to a simmer. Cook for 8–10 minutes.

3. Remove crabs from water and clean as follows. Lift off the hard shell and discard. Remove spongy gills. Rinse crabs and cut each into 4–6 sections (each section should have 2–3 legs attached). Most of the meaty bits are at the body section of the legs.

4. Heat a large electric frying pan, wok or large pan with a lid. Add butter and garlic, then crab, wine and ginger (if using). Cover and boil rapidly for 5 minutes, stirring the crab from time to time for even cooking.

5. Remove the lid, season with pepper and add spring onion. Replace lid and toss well. Bibs and plenty of bread are a must.

DID YOU KNOW?

Male paddle crabs share a courting technique with cicadas. The crab rubs its leg against a rasp under its claw, 'stridulating' to attract a mate.

Seafood crêpes

SERVES 4 | Recipe by Colin Doyle

This is a very versatile dish and a great way of using up any leftover seafood. The sauce uses fish stock rather than milk to make a slightly lighter filling. Try using tortillas (see recipe page 272) rather than crêpes for a super-quick and easy meal. A few salad leaves on the side and a nice glass of Riesling are sure to make this a favourite.

CRÊPES

½ cup plain flour

2 eggs

2 tbsp melted butter

½ cup milk

¼ cup tepid water

½ tsp salt

FILLING

30g butter

2 tbsp plain flour

1 cup fish stock (see recipe page 272), warm

300g marinara mix, well drained

100g raw prawn meat, roughly chopped

50g scallops, sliced

1 cup grated Cheddar

2 tbsp each chopped fresh chives, tarragon and parsley

Butter for frying

1. To make crêpes, combine all ingredients in a food processor or whisk by hand. Allow to rest for 20 minutes. Batter should be quite thin and easily poured.

2. Preheat oven to 180°C.

3. To make the filling, melt butter in a pan and add flour. Cook for approximately 4 minutes or until it is lightly coloured and fragrant. Slowly whisk in stock and stir until thick.

4. Grease a non-stick pan or crêpe pan with a little butter and cook crêpes one at a time, lifting the pan off the heat while adding the batter and swirling the pan to get a very thin, even coating over the bottom of the pan. Cook crêpes until the top is set and the outer edge is beginning to show lacy brown fringes. Turn the crêpe with a spatula or your fingers and cook until the second side is lightly browned. Lightly grease the pan and repeat until batter is all used up. You should get 10–12 crêpes. Set crêpes aside until sauce is finished.

5. Add marinara mix, prawn meat and scallops to the sauce. Cook for 2 minutes and remove from heat. Stir in half the grated cheese and the chopped herbs.

6. Lay one crêpe in the centre of a large ovenproof dish and place on about 2 tablespoons of filling. Roll crêpe into a cigar shape and move to the end of the dish. Fill remaining crêpes in a similar manner. Distribute any remaining filling over crêpes and top with remaining grated cheese. Bake until cheese bubbles and turns golden brown, approximately 20 minutes.

Open prawn wontons

SERVES 4 AS A STARTER | Recipe by Mark Dronjak

Dinner party sophistication.

Light vegetable oil, for frying
Avocado oil, for frying (and to add colour)
8 wonton wrappers (thicker variety), cut in half
    on the diagonal to form triangles
125g cream cheese
Lime-infused avocado oil
Sea salt and freshly ground pepper
½–1 red chilli, deseeded (optional) and finely diced
Splash of cider vinegar
1 avocado, halved and thinly sliced
175g cooked small–medium prawns
75g water chestnuts, sliced

1. In a pan heat enough of each of the two oils to lightly fry, one at a time, the wonton wrappers until crisp and just coloured. When cooked, place on paper towels.

2. Combine cream cheese with a little lime-infused avocado oil. Season to taste.

3. To make the dressing, combine chilli, cider vinegar and some lime-infused avocado oil. Season to taste.

4. To assemble the dish, spread a little cream cheese mixture in the middle of 4 plates, then place one of the wonton triangles on top of each. Layer each with another spread of cream cheese, avocado, prawns and a slice or two of water chestnut. Place a wonton triangle on top and repeat the process. Drizzle dressing over the wontons and around the plates. Garnish with remaining water chestnuts.

Crispy alfonsino, chorizo and chickpea salad ▶

SERVES 4 | Recipe by Petra New

It's always important to add texture to your food; the chickpeas in this salad do just that.

2 chorizo sausages, sliced
4 alfonsino fillets, boned, skin on
Salt and freshly ground pepper
1 tsp wholegrain mustard
1 tbsp white balsamic vinegar
1 clove garlic, crushed
Zest and segments of 1 orange
150ml oil
100g baby spinach leaves, washed
¼ red onion, sliced
½ yellow capsicum, sliced
200g canned chickpeas, washed and drained

1. Place a pan over medium heat and sauté chorizo until browned. Remove from heat and drain on a paper towel.

2. Return pan to the heat and place fish skin-side down in the pan to cook in the oil from the chorizo. When the skin is crispy and browned, turn the fish. Season and cook for a further 3 minutes.

3. To make dressing, whisk together mustard, vinegar, garlic, orange zest and oil. Season to taste.

4. Combine spinach, red onion, chorizo, capsicum, orange segments and chickpeas in a bowl and toss with the dressing.

5. To serve, divide salad among 4 plates, then top with fish fillets.

Baby Mediterranean fishcakes with tzatziki

SERVES 4 | Recipe by Petra New

An easy way to stretch the food budget while ensuring you incorporate fish in your diet.

TZATZIKI

100g thick Greek yoghurt

¼ cup finely diced telegraph cucumber, seeds removed

2 cloves garlic, crushed

2 tbsp chopped fresh mint

400g white fish fillets (e.g. gurnard), skinned and pin-boned

½ red onion, finely diced

2 tbsp sun-dried tomatoes, thinly sliced

4 black olives, pitted and chopped

1 tbsp chopped fresh basil

Salt and freshly ground pepper

1 egg

1 slice day-old bread, processed to make crumbs

Olive oil

1. To make tzatziki, mix together all ingredients and allow flavours to infuse for at least 15 minutes before serving.

2. Roughly dice fish and place in a food processor. Pulse until just minced. Do not over-process fish as it will become rubbery.

3. Transfer to a mixing bowl. Add onion, sun-dried tomatoes, olives, basil, salt and pepper and mix gently with your fingertips. Add egg to combine and then a small amount of breadcrumbs, a little at a time to make sure the mix does not become too dry.

4. Roll into 12 balls using approximately 1½ tablespoons of the mixture for each and then gently pat flat to form a disc shape.

5. Place a pan over medium heat, add a dash of olive oil and fry fishcakes a few at a time for 2 minutes. Turn and fry for another 2 minutes. Drain on paper towels.

6. To serve, place 3 fishcakes on each plate, top with tzatziki and drizzle with olive oil.

COOK'S NOTE

These fishcakes can also be cooked on the barbecue, or lightly brushed with olive oil and baked in a 200°C oven for 5 minutes.

Smoked salmon, leek and beer fritters with garlic mayonnaise

SERVES 4 | Recipe by Petra New

Make sure you use a light-flavoured beer so the taste is not too strong.

GARLIC MAYONNAISE

2 egg yolks

1 clove garlic, crushed

1 tsp Dijon mustard

Juice of 1 lemon

200ml soy or canola oil

Salt and white pepper

300g hot-smoked salmon fillet

½ leek, diced

¼ medium onion, diced

1 cup plain flour

1 tsp baking powder

½ tsp salt

Pinch of white pepper

¼ cup flat-leaf parsley, chopped

2 eggs

300ml lager or other mild-flavoured beer

Soy or canola oil

1 lemon, cut into wedges

1. To make garlic mayonnaise, whisk together egg yolks, garlic, mustard and lemon juice in a very clean bowl until lightened in colour. Start drizzling in oil very slowly so as not to 'split' the mayonnaise while whisking. When you have added all the oil, taste and season. For a creamy, thinner consistency, whisk in 1–2 tablespoons of warm water.

2. Flake salmon into a bowl, removing any bones.

3. Heat a pan over medium heat and sauté leek and onion until soft. Remove from the heat and cool.

4. Sift flour, baking powder, salt and pepper together into a bowl. Add parsley, flaked salmon and leek and onion mix, and lightly blend. Make a well in the centre into which to crack the eggs, then pour in half the beer and with a fork whisk the egg and beer together. Using a large metal spoon, start to fold all ingredients together, adding remaining beer as required. The fritters will be lighter if you do not over-mix.

5. Heat barbecue to a medium–low heat and place a barbecue liner on the flat plate. Drizzle liner with oil.

6. Drop on tablespoon-sized dollops of fritter mix, spreading slightly with the back of the spoon. When bubbles start to form and pop, turn over and cook for the same amount of time as you did for the first side.

7. To serve, place 3 fritters onto each plate. Serve with a ramekin of garlic mayonnaise and a wedge of lemon.

Prawn and papaya salad with lemongrass dressing

SERVES 4 | Recipe by Petra New

Summer on a plate! Remember when you dress the salad that everything should be coated, but there shouldn't be a puddle of liquid at the bottom of the bowl. Over-dressing ruins any good salad.

24 large raw prawns, shelled

Zest and juice of 1 lime

2 cloves garlic, crushed

1cm fresh ginger, grated

1 firm papaya, diced

¼ iceberg lettuce, shredded

1 cup bean sprouts

2 tbsp chopped fresh mint

2 tbsp chopped fresh coriander

LEMONGRASS DRESSING

Juice of 2 limes

1 tbsp fish sauce

1 tsp grated dark palm sugar

1 tbsp pickled ginger, shredded

2 tbsp sweet chilli sauce

5cm stalk lemongrass, finely chopped

2 tbsp peanut oil

Salt and freshly ground pepper

¼ cup cashew nuts, roasted and chopped, for garnish

1. Place prawns in a bowl with lime zest and juice. Add garlic and ginger and marinate for 5 minutes.

2. In another bowl, mix together papaya, lettuce, bean sprouts, mint and coriander. Set aside.

3. To make lemongrass dressing, place second measure of lime juice in a jug. Mix in fish sauce and palm sugar until the palm sugar dissolves. Add pickled ginger, sweet chilli sauce and lemongrass. Set aside.

4. Heat peanut oil in a pan over medium–high heat. Shake excess liquid off prawns (reserving marinade), then add to pan. Sauté until bright orange/pink and season to taste. Pour over marinade and cook for 30 seconds. Remove from heat.

5. Toss dressing through salad – always do this just before serving to make sure the salad stays crisp. You may not need all of the dressing.

6. To serve, arrange salad on each plate in a high heap, garnish with 6 prawns and drizzle over pan juices. Garnish with chopped cashew nuts.

Mussel, coconut and tamarind salad

SERVES 4 | Recipe by Steve Roberts

A truly stunning Vietnamese salad combining succulent mussels with creamy coconut and tart tamarind – and oh-so-easy to prepare. Serve on a banana leaf for extra flair.

HOT AND SOUR DRESSING

100ml lime juice

2 tbsp fish sauce

2 red chillies, deseeded and finely chopped

40g caster sugar

2kg mussels, cleaned

200ml white wine

1 stalk lemongrass, finely sliced

80ml tamarind water

3 Kaffir lime leaves, finely shredded

1.5cm piece fresh ginger, finely grated

5 shallots, finely sliced

½ cup coconut thread, lightly toasted

2 red chillies, deseeded (optional) and finely sliced

Good handful of fresh coriander leaves

Good handful of fresh mint leaves

½ cup peanuts, roughly chopped

2 tbsp salmon caviar (optional)

150g fried shallots (available from Asian supermarkets)

1. To make hot and sour dressing, mix together all dressing ingredients in a small bowl or jar until combined.

2. In a lidded saucepan, steam mussels in white wine with lemongrass for approximately 2 minutes, until open. Discard cooking liquor and remove mussels from the shell, removing and discarding foot and beard.

3. Combine dressing and tamarind water in a bowl. Add the mussels and marinate for 5 minutes.

4. Add Kaffir lime leaves, ginger, shallots, coconut, chillies, coriander, mint, peanuts and salmon caviar (if using), and gently combine.

5. Serve in a bowl garnished with fried shallots.

DID YOU KNOW?

One 100-gram serving of green-lipped mussels provides a quarter of an adult's daily protein needs and just under half the daily iodine they require.

Seared scallops with vanilla leek and pineapple and melon salsa

SERVES 4 | Recipe by Marco Edwardes

Fresh and light – great for those long lunches shared with friends.

PINEAPPLE AND MELON SALSA

1 tbsp honey
150g fresh pineapple, diced
150g rock melon, diced
½ tsp Madras curry powder
Salt and freshly ground pepper

1 leek
50g butter
Pinch of sugar
½ vanilla bean, seeds scraped
Salt and freshly ground pepper
Olive oil
350g scallops, washed and dried
Juice of 2 lemons
Chopped fresh coriander and mint,
    for garnish

1. To make pineapple and melon salsa, place honey in a small pan and gently heat. Add pineapple and rock melon. Season with curry powder, salt and pepper, then set aside until required.

2. Wash leek and cut into fine julienne.

3. Melt butter in a small pan. Add sugar and vanilla seeds. Add leek and sauté until soft. Season and set aside until required.

4. Just before serving, heat a medium-sized frying pan and add a little olive oil. When the oil is hot, add scallops. Sear scallops quickly until golden brown on both sides (being careful not to overcook). Season to taste and finish with a squeeze of lemon juice.

5. Arrange vanilla leek as a base on scallop shells or on plates and place seared scallops on top. Finish with pineapple and melon salsa. Garnish with coriander and mint.

Pasta, rice and noodles

Paella 110

Two-cheese tortellini with seared scallops and tomato and basil dressing 112

Prawn and squid noodle box 114

Pan-fried cod on risotto 115

Open ravioli with snapper 115

Red wine risotto with sautéed squid and seasonal white fish 116

Kedgeree 118

Nasi goreng 119

Teriyaki salmon with somen noodle salad 120

Fettuccine with seasonal seafood, rocket and lemon 122

Asian herb and chilli linguine with marinated salmon skewers 123

Crispy-skinned alfonsino with creamy sweetcorn and crab risotto 124

Thai vegetable rice noodles 126

Clams with spaghetti, saffron and leek 126

Tortellini of prawns, fish and mushrooms in seafood citrus broth 129

Paella

SERVES 4–6 | Recipe by Shane Walsh

The perfect one-pan meal – packed full of flavour.

½ cup white wine
1 small red onion, chopped
12 mussels, cleaned
½ cup olive oil
1 chicken breast, skin on
12 raw prawn cutlets
100g squid rings
100g white fish fillet (e.g. gurnard), skinned and cut into bite-sized portions
1 small red onion, finely chopped
4 rashers bacon, finely chopped
4 cloves garlic, peeled and chopped
1 red capsicum, deseeded and finely chopped
400g can chopped tomatoes
90g chorizo sausage, thinly sliced
1 tsp cayenne pepper
Salt and freshly ground pepper
1 cup long-grain rice
2 cups chicken stock, heated
Pinch of saffron threads, soaked in water (optional)
2 tbsp chopped fresh parsley

1. Heat wine and onion in a large lidded pan. Add mussels, cover and gently shake pan for 4–5 minutes over high heat. After 3 minutes, start removing opened mussels and set aside. At the end of 5 minutes, discard any unopened mussels. Strain and reserve cooking liquid.

2. Set aside a few mussels in the shells for garnish. When mussels are cool, shell the remaining mussels, remove the foot and beard and cut meat into bite-sized pieces.

3. Heat half the oil in a large frying pan. Pat chicken dry with paper towels and sear it, skin-side down, until golden brown. Do not cook entirely, just enough to brown the skin. Remove from pan and set aside. When cool, cut into bite-sized pieces.

4. Add prawns, squid and fish to the pan and cook for 1 minute. Remove from pan and set aside.

5. Heat remaining oil in the pan. Add onion, bacon, garlic and capsicum and cook for 5 minutes or until the onion is soft. Add tomatoes, chorizo and cayenne. Season to taste. Stir in reserved mussel cooking liquid. Add rice and mix well. Add hot stock and mix again. Bring slowly to the boil. Reduce heat to low and simmer, uncovered, for 15 minutes without stirring. Stir through saffron (if using).

6. Place chicken, prawns, squid and fish on top of rice. Using a wooden spoon, push pieces into rice, then cover and cook over low heat for 10–15 minutes or until rice is tender and chicken and seafood are cooked. Add mussels for the last 2 minutes to heat.

7. Serve in the pan, garnished with whole mussels and with parsley on the side to sprinkle over.

Two-cheese tortellini with seared scallops and tomato and basil dressing

SERVES 4 | Recipe by Steve Roberts

A combination of flavours that will set your tastebuds alight.

130g chèvre goat's cheese

80g strong Cheddar, grated

2 tsp finely chopped chives

Pinch of cracked pepper

100g fresh egg pasta dough (see recipe page 272) or wonton wrappers

TOMATO AND BASIL DRESSING

3 large vine tomatoes, deseeded and finely chopped

Handful of fresh basil leaves

100ml olive oil

50ml balsamic vinegar

Sea salt and freshly ground pepper

Pinch sugar (optional)

20 scallops

Salt and freshly ground pepper

1 tbsp light olive oil

Micro greens, for garnish

1. Mix together goat's cheese, cheddar, chives and pepper.

2. If using pasta dough, using a pasta rolling machine that is well dusted with flour, roll pasta through the highest setting. Fold pasta into thirds and put through the next lowest setting. Repeat this process until you get through to the lowest setting.

3. Using a 5cm round cutter cut out 16 discs from pasta sheet (or wonton wrappers, if using). Place three-quarters of a teaspoon of cheese filling onto each round.

4. Fold rounds over to make a half moon shape. Bring the two edges together and seal by pinching between your fingers.

5. Place tortellini into a pot of boiling, well-salted water. Poach for 2 minutes, then remove and refresh in ice-cold water.

6. To make tomato and basil dressing, combine all ingredients and season to taste. If you find it a little sharp, add a pinch of sugar.

7. Season scallops and sauté them in a hot pan with a little oil for approximately 1 minute on each side. Remove from pan and rest scallops for a minute.

8. Gently reheat tortellini in a pot of simmering water for just a few seconds.

9. To serve, arrange scallops and tortellini evenly among 4 shallow serving bowls. Spoon over dressing and garnish with micro greens.

Prawn and squid noodle box

SERVES 4 | Recipe by John Campbell

Enjoy the flavours of a noodle box at home, perhaps as a relaxed weekend meal shared with family in front of a good movie. Great with any mix of your favourite seafood.

50ml sesame oil

400g prawn meat

1 squid tube, sliced

3 cloves garlic, chopped

2 spring onions, sliced

1 hot chilli, deseeded and chopped

3cm piece fresh ginger, chopped

250g can dark mushrooms, sliced

400g can sliced baby corn or bamboo
    shoots, cut in strips

4 bunches of bird nest egg noodles

Juice of 1 lime

1½ tbsp soy sauce

3 tbsp sweet chilli sauce

1 tbsp fish sauce

2 tbsp chopped fresh coriander

Sea salt and freshly ground pepper

50g crispy fried onions, for garnish
    (available from Asian supermarkets)

50g roasted cashews, for garnish

1. Heat a wok until hot. Add half the oil and sauté prawn meat for a few minutes, until pink. Remove from the pan and set aside. Next quickly sauté squid – taking care not to overcook. Remove from pan and set aside.

2. Add the rest of the oil to the pan and sauté garlic, spring onion, chilli and ginger. Add mushrooms and corn or bamboo shoots.

3. Blanch noodles in boiling seasoned water for 4–5 minutes. Add noodles to sauté mix, along with all other ingredients (except fried onions and cashews). Mix well.

4. Serve in noodle boxes with chopsticks. Garnish with fried onions and roasted cashews.

Pan-fried cod on risotto

SERVES 4 | Recipe by John Campbell

Serve as a light lunch with salad or rocket leaves.

RISOTTO

50ml extra virgin olive oil

½ onion, finely diced

2 cloves garlic, chopped

300g Arborio rice

50ml white wine

700ml chicken stock

Salt and freshly ground pepper

2 tbsp chopped fresh basil

2 tbsp chopped fresh parsley

50g Parmesan, grated

30ml extra virgin olive oil

4 × 100g cod fillets

50g crème fraîche, to serve

20g preserved lemon (see recipe page 271), skin only, to serve

1. To make risotto, heat a large pot and add oil. Gently cook onion and garlic until translucent. Add rice and stir to coat with oil.

2. Add wine and cook for about 20 minutes, stirring through 150ml of stock every few minutes. Season to taste. Add basil, parsley and Parmesan.

3. Heat oil in a sauté pan. Season then pan-fry cod on both sides for 4–5 minutes.

4. To serve, divide risotto among 4 plates and top with fish, a little crème fraîche and preserved lemon.

Open ravioli with snapper

SERVES 4 AS A STARTER | Recipe by Mark Dronjak

Ravioli with character.

4 fresh pasta sheets (store-bought or see recipe page 272)

50g butter

2 tbsp olive oil

300g snapper fillet (or gurnard or smoked kahawai), diced

75ml fresh cream

100g fresh ricotta cheese

12 small chives, finely chopped

Sea salt and white pepper

Truffle-infused olive oil for drizzling

Juice of 2 lemons

75g Pecorino cheese, freshly shaved

Handful of flat-leaf parsley leaves, for garnish

1. Lay the pasta sheets on the bench and cut into 8 rounds or squares of your prefered size with a suitable cutter.

2. To make the filling, heat butter and oil in a small pan. Add snapper and cook until just done. Do not overcook. Add cream, ricotta and most of the chives. Season to taste.

3. Cook pasta in boiling salted water for 4–6 minutes, then drain well and pat dry with a paper towel, if needed.

4. To serve, place one round of pasta on each plate. Arrange snapper filling in the middle of pasta and drizzle with a little truffle-infused olive oil. Position another pasta round on top and sprinkle with lemon juice, remaining chives and shaved Pecorino. Garnish with parsley leaves.

Red wine risotto with sautéed squid and seasonal white fish

SERVES 4 | Recipe by John Campbell

A stunning-looking dish topped with grilled seafood and vegetables.

300g squid tubes, sliced

2 cloves garlic, chopped

Zest and juice of 1 lemon

2 tbsp extra virgin olive oil

2 courgettes, cut into strips

RISOTTO

50ml extra virgin olive oil

½ onion, finely diced

2 cloves garlic, chopped

250g Arborio rice

200ml red wine

400ml chicken stock

Salt

New York cut black pepper (see glossary page 276)

2 tbsp chopped fresh sage

2 tbsp chopped fresh parsley

50g Parmesan, grated

Oil for frying

320g seasonal white fish fillets (e.g. monkfish, hapuku), skinned and cut into chunks

1. Coat squid in garlic, lemon zest and juice and oil, reserving a little oil for cooking. Add courgette strips to the marinade and leave for 20 minutes.

2. To make risotto, heat a large pot and add oil. Gently cook onion and garlic until translucent. Add rice and cook for a few minutes (do not allow it to colour). Add wine and cook for a few minutes further. Continue cooking rice mix for about 18 minutes, adding the stock one third at a time every 5 minutes. Season. Add herbs and Parmesan.

3. In another pan, heated to very hot, sauté marinated squid and courgettes quickly, taking care not to overcook squid. Season to taste.

4. Pan-fry fish fillets for a few minutes on each side in a little oil.

5. To serve, portion the risotto into 4 bowls. Top with the sautéed squid, courgettes and fish.

Kedgeree

SERVES 4 | Recipe by Colin Doyle

A Victorian breakfast classic, usually made with smoked haddock, updated for twenty-first-century Kiwi tastes using our wonderful South Island salmon.

50g butter
1 tsp mustard seeds
1 tbsp curry powder
2 cardamom pods
1 small onion, finely diced
1 cup long-grain rice (preferably Basmati)
1 cup milk
1 cup fish stock (see recipe page 272)
1 bunch fresh curry leaves
1 tomato, deseeded and finely diced
⅓ cup frozen peas
Pinch of grated nutmeg
4 hard-boiled eggs, quartered
¼ cup coconut cream
300g hot-smoked salmon, flaked
Small bunch fresh coriander, chopped
Small bunch fresh parsley, chopped
Salt and freshly ground pepper
1 lemon, cut into wedges

1. Melt butter in a pan; add mustard seeds and cook for a few seconds until they begin to pop.

2. Add curry powder and cardamom pods, stir to cook briefly, and then add diced onion.

3. When onion begins to soften, add rice, mixing it to get an even coating. Add milk and fish stock along with the curry leaves and tomato. Simmer for 10–15 minutes or until the rice begins to soften, stirring occasionally. You may need to add a little water if the mixture looks to be drying out.

4. When rice is tender, add frozen peas, nutmeg, eggs, coconut cream and flaked salmon. Allow to warm through, then stir through coriander and parsley. Remove curry leaves and discard. Adjust seasoning to taste.

5. Serve topped with lemon wedges.

Nasi goreng

SERVES 4 | Recipe by Colin Doyle

There are many variations to this Indonesian classic. Some cooks serve the rice topped with a fried egg, while others serve it with a shredded omelette. Prawns are used here, but mussels, scallops and squid also work well.

50ml vegetable oil

3 eggs, lightly beaten (divided into 2 lots)

1 tsp shrimp paste

2 cloves garlic, minced

1 tsp sambal oelek or 1 red chilli, deseeded (optional) and diced

2cm piece fresh ginger, minced

1 shallot, finely diced

400g raw prawn meat

½ tsp curry powder

⅓ tsp ground nutmeg

3 cups cold cooked rice

¼ tsp white pepper

½ cup mung bean sprouts

3 tbsp kecap manis

⅓ cup roasted peanuts, roughly chopped

½ telegraph cucumber, thinly sliced

1. Heat one-third of the oil in a wok and when hot add half the beaten egg, rolling it round the rim to make a thin omelette. Transfer omelette to a board and prepare a second omelette with remainder of the egg. Allow omelettes to cool slightly, then roll each into a cylinder and thinly slice. Set aside.

2. Heat half the remaining oil in the wok and quickly fry shrimp paste, then add garlic, sambal oelek or chilli, ginger and shallot. Add prawn meat and cook for 1 minute. Transfer prawn mix to a bowl.

3. Heat remaining oil and fry curry powder and nutmeg until aromatic. Add the cooked rice and mix until rice has heated through. Return prawn mix to the wok along with sliced omelette. Season with white pepper. Stir in bean sprouts and kecap manis.

4. Serve topped with chopped peanuts and cucumber slices on the side.

COOK'S NOTE
You can remove the seeds and membrane of the chilli before chopping if you prefer a milder taste.

Teriyaki salmon with somen noodle salad

SERVES 4 | Recipe by Steve Roberts

This is a lovely light dish, great for a starter or an easy summer lunch.

TERIYAKI SAUCE

120ml soy sauce

100ml mirin

100ml sake

⅓ cup caster sugar

50ml rice wine vinegar

1 tsp finely grated ginger

60ml mirin

1½ tbsp tamari

150g somen noodles

1 cucumber, finely julienned

1 tbsp chopped fresh chives

2 tbsp sesame seeds

1 tsp red chilli flakes

4 × 150g salmon (or kingfish) fillets, pin-boned, skin on

Oil for frying

1. To make teriyaki sauce, mix all ingredients in a bowl until sugar has dissolved.

2. In another bowl combine vinegar, ginger, mirin and tamari and mix to make the dressing for the salad.

3. Cook somen noodles until al dente. Refresh in cold water, then drain well.

4. Add dressing to noodles along with cucumber, chives, sesame seeds and chilli flakes. Toss to combine.

5. Sear salmon fillets in a hot pan in a little oil, skin-side down, and turn after approximately 1 minute. When almost cooked, add teriyaki sauce and reduce until it becomes syrupy and glazes the salmon.

6. To serve, arrange some noodle salad in the centre of each plate and top with a salmon fillet, then drizzle plates with remaining teriyaki sauce from the pan.

DID YOU KNOW?

The Mackenzie Basin in the Southern Alps is home to a unique system of freshwater salmon farming, using the lakes and canals associated with the hydroelectric dams there. One of the farms, at 677 metres, is the highest salmon farm in the world.

Fettuccine with seasonal seafood, rocket and lemon

SERVES 4 | Recipe by Mark Dronjak

Mamma mia . . . Italian cuisine featuring the 'pick of the sea'.

200g fresh fettuccine pasta

Olive oil

2 cloves garlic, finely crushed

1 medium white onion, finely chopped

12 cockles, purged

100ml white wine

150ml fish stock (see recipe page 272)

150ml fresh cream

50g butter

150g squid tubes, cut into pieces

200g raw prawn meat

100g rocket leaves

200g fresh white fish fillets (monkfish is ideal), cut into cubes

Juice of 2 lemons

Zest of ½–1 lemon

Sea salt and ground white pepper

Flat-leaf parsley, roughly chopped, for garnish

75g Parmesan, freshly grated

1. Cook fettuccine in boiling salted water until al dente. Drain well. Toss fettuccine with a little olive oil and keep warm in the same pan. The key is to get the entire dish ready at the same time to avoid pasta sitting around for too long.

2. In a separate large pan, heat a little olive oil. Add garlic and onion. Cook for a few moments without colouring then add cockles, stirring occasionally until they have opened. (Placing a lid on the pan will assist.) When cockles have opened, remove them from the pan and keep warm.

3. To the same pan, add wine, stock and cream and reduce slightly. Add butter, squid and prawn meat and rocket. Bring to a gentle simmer.

4. Add fish and continue to gently simmer for a few minutes. Add half the lemon juice and all the zest. Return opened cockles to the pan. Check seasoning.

5. Add pasta to the pan and combine the ingredients well, taking care not to break up the seafood.

6. Serve on a large platter or in pasta bowls. Sprinkle with parsley and Parmesan. Add the remaining lemon juice if required, and serve with crusty bread.

Asian herb and chilli linguine with marinated salmon skewers

SERVES 4 | Recipe by Steve Roberts

A simple yet elegant dish bursting with the flavour of fresh herbs and chilli and finished with a sweet soy glaze. A true balance of flavours.

ASIAN HERB AND CHILLI LINGUINE

120g linguine, fresh or dried

1 large red chilli, deseeded (optional) and finely sliced

2 tsp fish sauce

Handful of fresh mint leaves

Handful of fresh basil leaves

Handful of fresh coriander leaves

1 spring onion, julienned

1 tbsp extra virgin olive oil

Sea salt and freshly ground pepper

MARINATED SALMON SKEWERS

8 × 40g salmon fillets (or kingfish, monkfish or broadbill)

5cm piece of fresh ginger, peeled and minced

5cm piece of lemongrass, minced

Zest and juice of 1 lime

2 tbsp canola oil

60ml mirin

70ml tbsp low-sodium soy sauce

1 tbsp kecap manis, to finish

1. Place 8 bamboo skewers in water to soak.

2. Cook linguine until al dente, drain well and toss with chilli, fish sauce, herbs, spring onion and olive oil. Season to taste.

3. Thread salmon onto skewers.

4. Combine ginger, lemongrass, lime zest and juice, oil, mirin and soy sauce and marinate salmon in the mix for around 10 minutes.

5. Drain off excess marinade. Sear salmon skewers over a high heat for a couple of minutes.

6. Arrange linguine in the centre of each serving plate and place salmon skewers on top. Finish with a drizzle of kecap manis.

Crispy-skinned alfonsino with creamy sweetcorn and crab risotto

SERVES 4 | Recipe by Steve Roberts

Alfonsino is an underrated fish, but given a nice crispy skin and teamed with a sweetcorn and crab risotto it is sublime.

CREAMY SWEETCORN AND CRAB RISOTTO

2 tbsp finely diced shallots

50ml extra virgin olive oil

80g Arborio rice

100ml dry white wine

800ml fish stock (see recipe page 272)

40–50g spanner crabmeat

20g cold butter, cut into 1cm cubes

1 tbsp mascarpone

2 tbsp grated Parmesan

200g sweetcorn kernels

Handful of fresh chives, chopped

Salt and freshly ground pepper

4 × 180g fillets alfonsino, skin on and boned (any species of white fish can be used)

Salt and freshly ground pepper

Oil for frying

Pea shoots, for garnish

1. To make creamy sweetcorn and crab risotto, sauté shallots in olive oil in a deep, heavy-based pot, over a very low heat. Stir with a wooden spoon and do not allow shallots to colour.

2. Add rice. Stir continuously to coat rice with the olive oil. Add wine and reduce until liquid has almost disappeared.

3. Use a ladle to add stock, a little at a time. Only stir rice occasionally and gently, and add more stock as it is absorbed. Mix in crabmeat.

4. Test rice by eating a grain or two. It should be soft but with a slight crunch or bite in the centre. Move the pot to the side of the stove.

5. Add butter, cheeses, sweetcorn kernels and chives. Gently fold through rice and season to taste. Add a little more stock to get a really smooth and creamy finish.

6. Season alfonsino. Sear in a hot pan skin-side down in a little oil to crisp it. Turn fish over and turn off heat. Allow to finish cooking for a few minutes and then set aside to rest.

7. To serve, spoon a little risotto into the centre of each serving plate. Place a cooked fillet on top with crispy skin facing up. Garnish with pea shoots.

Thai vegetable rice noodles

SERVES 4 AS A SIDE DISH | Recipe by Petra New

Great served alongside freshly cooked fish fillets.

3 tbsp peanut oil

4 cloves garlic, crushed

1 shallot, diced

200g fresh rice noodles (available from Asian supermarkets)

150ml good-quality chicken stock

2 tbsp crushed palm sugar

2 tbsp fish sauce

1 tbsp soy sauce

3 tbsp tamarind juice

½ cup bean sprouts

1 cup shredded cabbage

1 carrot, grated

¼ cup roasted peanuts, roughly chopped, for garnish

1 lime, cut into wedges, to serve

1. Place peanut oil in a wok over a high heat; when hot, stir-fry garlic and shallot.

2. Add noodles. Continue to stir-fry, always keeping the wok on a high heat.

3. Mix in stock, palm sugar, fish sauce, soy sauce and tamarind juice. Stir-fry for another few minutes.

4. Add bean sprouts, cabbage and carrot. Stir until vegetables have just wilted.

5. Place on a serving plate and garnish with peanuts and lime wedges.

Clams with spaghetti, saffron and leek ▶

SERVES 4–6 | Recipe by Marco Edwardes

A taste of Italy – quick, simple and delicious.

20g butter

2 tbsp olive oil

1 leek, washed well and thinly sliced

4 cloves garlic, crushed

125ml white wine

½ cup chicken stock

1 cup cream

Large pinch of saffron threads, soaked in 50ml warm water

1kg clams, purged

400g good-quality spaghetti

2 tsp chopped fresh dill

3 tbsp chopped fresh parsley

Juice of ½ lemon

Sea salt and freshly ground pepper

1. Heat butter and oil in a large lidded saucepan then add leek and garlic and cook, stirring occasionally, over low heat for 10 minutes or until soft. Add wine and increase heat to medium. Cook until reduced by half.

2. Add chicken stock, cream and saffron mixture and simmer for 10 minutes or until sauce begins to thicken. Add clams, cover and cook for 5–8 minutes or until clams open. Discard any unopened clams.

3. Meanwhile, cook spaghetti in plenty of boiling salted water until al dente, then drain well.

4. Stir dill, parsley and lemon juice into clam mixture, season to taste, add spaghetti and toss gently to combine.

5. Serve in shallow bowls.

Tortellini of prawns, fish and mushrooms in seafood citrus broth

SERVES 4 | Recipe by Steve Roberts

A fantastic one-bowl meal that covers all bases – vegetables, seafood and broth.

TORTELLINI
(MAKES APPROXIMATELY 30)
4 fresh shiitake mushrooms
125g raw prawn meat
125g white fish, (e.g. gurnard)
Handful of chopped fresh basil
Handful of chopped flat-leaf parsley
Sea salt and freshly ground pepper
Approximately 30 wonton wrappers
1 egg, beaten with 1 tbsp milk

SEAFOOD CITRUS BROTH
1 tsp olive oil
1 leek, white part only, finely sliced
Zest of 2 limes and 2 lemons
1 litre fish stock (see recipe page 272)
2 bay leaves
½ celery, diced
Pinch of saffron, soaked in a little water
1 sprig of fresh thyme

2 large ripe tomatoes, deseeded and diced
1 bunch spinach leaves, washed and stems
    removed, thinly sliced
Fresh coriander leaves, for garnish

1. To make tortellini, roughly chop mushrooms and prawn and fish meat. Briefly process in a food processor. Add basil, parsley and seasoning and pulse.

2. Poach a little of the filling in hot water to test the seasoning and adjust if necessary.

3. Lay out wonton wrappers. Cut into rounds and brush edges with egg mix. Place a teaspoon of filling in the centre of each wrapper. Fold into a tortellini shape, ensuring all sides are well sealed, then set aside.

4. To make seafood citrus broth, heat oil in a large pan and gently cook the leeks with the lime and lemon zests until soft. Add stock, bay leaves, celery, saffron and thyme and simmer for 20 minutes. Remove from heat and strain, removing bay leaves.

5. Gently poach tortellini in simmering salted water (poaching in the broth would make it cloudy).

6. To serve, divide tomato, spinach leaves and coriander between serving bowls along with the tortellini, making sure they are evenly portioned out, and pour over hot broth.

Barbecues
and grills

Barbecued seafood platter with charred vegetables and rosemary potatoes   132

Barbecue-seared five-spice squid with wasabi aioli   134

Grilled fish fillets with bok choy and mandarin and ginger sauce   136

Barbecued black bean salmon fillet on ginger and sesame vegetables   137

Barbecued fish with hot and sour chilli sauce   138

Chargrilled fish fillets with balsamic mushrooms   138

Barbecued chilli squid with Asian spices and green beans   140

Grilled fish fillets with chilli jam-spiced eggplant relish and green beans   143

Mediterranean-style grilled scampi   144

Crispy tiger prawns with lime and chilli   144

Whole barbecue-grilled market fish with Greek potato mash   146

Chargrilled maple and apple salmon steaks, baked potatoes and fennel slaw   148

Ginger and manuka honey-glazed hot-smoked kahawai with avocado salsa   149

Orange and sage barbecued mussels   150

Grilled prawns with tomato, feta and dill   150

Grilled crayfish   152

Barbecued sticky Chinese orange and ginger snapper parcels   154

Barbecued bluenose on crushed potatoes with caper, lemon and olive dressing   155

Bruschetta with seared octopus   156

Grilled flounder   156

Ultimate seafood mixed grill   158

Kasbah mussels with tomatoes, coriander, olives and capsicum   159

Hot-smoked salmon with potato cakes and beurre blanc   160

Fish burgers   162

Barbecued seafood platter with charred vegetables and rosemary potatoes

SERVES 4 | Recipe by John Campbell

An ideal platter-dish to share with friends.

CHARRED VEGETABLES

2 tbsp olive oil

½ eggplant, cut lengthwise, then cut across into medium slices

1 yellow capsicum, deseeded and thickly sliced

1 medium red onion, peeled and cut into wedges

1 large courgette, thickly sliced on an angle

4 cloves garlic, skin on

1 carrot, peeled and sliced on the angle

Handful of flat-leaf parsley and basil and 1–2 sprigs of thyme

Salt and freshly ground pepper

ROSEMARY POTATOES

200g Agria potatoes, washed, unpeeled

2 tbsp olive oil

1 sprig of rosemary

Salt and freshly ground pepper

300g squid tubes, sliced

1 garlic clove, crushed

50ml extra virgin olive oil

400g salmon, skin on, pin-boned

300g snapper

Salt and freshly ground pepper

Dukkah (see recipe page 260)

4 grilled lemon or lime halves (see recipe page 271), to serve

1. To make charred vegetables, rub two-thirds of the olive oil into the eggplant. Use remaining oil to rub into the other cut vegetables; keep the carrot separate as it takes longer to cook.

2. Char vegetables on the barbecue, but only put capsicum, garlic and eggplant on the grate as the smaller vegetables could fall through. The rest can be grilled on the hot plate or even sautéed in a wok. Remember to watch the heat and rotate the vegetables. Cook them until firm to the bite, then remove and cool on a tray. Mix in herbs and season to taste.

3. To make rosemary potatoes, slice potatoes into wedges and toss with olive oil, rosemary and seasoning. Grill potatoes on the hot plate for 10–12 minutes, turning from time to time for an even colour. Remove when soft but not mushy. To speed up the cooking time, pre-cook the potatoes.

4. Coat squid with crushed garlic and a drizzle of olive oil.

5. Brush or toss fish in some olive oil, roll the salmon in salt and pepper and the snapper in dukkah.

6. Place a barbecue liner on the barbecue hot plate.

7. Place fish on the hot plate to seal and squid on the grate. They will take only a few minutes to cook.

8. To serve, place vegetables on a platter, top with seafood and serve with potato wedges and grilled lemon or lime halves.

Barbecue-seared five-spice squid with wasabi aioli

SERVES 4 | Recipe by Mark Dronjak

Sesame, Chinese five spice and squid . . . perfect with the wasabi aioli.

600g squid tubes
3–4 tsp Chinese five spice
Flaky sea salt
3 tbsp sesame oil

WASABI AIOLI
2–3 tsp prepared wasabi paste, according
  to taste
Juice of ½ lemon
1 egg yolk
Pinch of caster sugar (optional)
150ml sunflower or good-quality
  vegetable oil
Salt and white pepper

2 sprigs flat-leaf parsley, for garnish
1 lemon, cut into wedges, to serve

1. Prepare squid tubes by cutting into rings or by cutting the tube in half and scoring the inside flesh with a small sharp knife, then cutting into 75–100mm wide pieces.

2. Place Chinese five spice in a bowl with a good sprinkle of sea salt and sesame oil. Add prepared squid to the bowl and stir to coat. Allow to marinate for 5–10 minutes.

3. To make wasabi aioli, whisk together wasabi paste, lemon juice, egg yolk and sugar (if using). Drizzle oil in very slowly – you may find you don't need to use the full amount of oil. Season to taste. Leave to settle prior to using, to allow the flavours to mellow.

4. Cook squid on a hot barbecue plate or grill until the squid starts to colour. Do not overcook or it will toughen.

5. Serve chargrilled squid with wasabi aioli on the side. Garnish with parsley sprigs and lemon wedges.

Grilled fish fillets with bok choy and mandarin and ginger sauce

SERVES 4 | Recipe by Marco Edwardes

A great dish to impress and a delicious sauce not to be rushed.

MANDARIN AND GINGER SAUCE

500g fresh mandarins

100ml orange juice

100ml fish stock (see recipe page 272)

100ml cream

Small piece of fresh ginger, grated

30g cold butter, diced

Salt and freshly ground pepper

Zest of 2 mandarins, julienned and
   blanched (optional)

4 small bok choy (or 2 large bok choy)

Olive oil

Pinch of salt

4 × 160g market-fresh white fish fillets,
   skin on

Sesame oil

20g white sesame seeds

20g black sesame seeds

Sea salt and freshly ground pepper

4 cups steamed rice, to serve

1. To make mandarin and ginger sauce, peel mandarins and place in a food processor. Blend to a pulp, then pass through a fine sieve.

2. Combine resulting mandarin juice, orange juice and fish stock in a small saucepan. Place over medium heat and reduce by half. Add cream and ginger. Gently boil for a few minutes until the sauce thickens and covers the back of a spoon. Pass through a sieve again.

3. Whisk in butter a little at a time to make a smooth, shiny sauce. Season to taste, then add mandarin zest (if using). Set sauce aside.

4. To prepare the bok choy, cut in half and remove middle stem. Wash under cold running water.

5. In a medium-sized saucepan bring water to the boil. Add salt and blanch bok choy for 1–2 minutes then refresh in cold water. Strain and dry bok choy. Set aside.

6. Heat a large frying pan over medium heat and add olive oil. Place fish skin-side down in the pan. Fry fish for 2 minutes skin-side down and then turn over and cook for a further 2 minutes or until cooked. Do not overcook. Transfer to a plate and cover with tin foil.

7. Sauté bok choy in a small frying pan with sesame oil and sesame seeds. Season to taste.

8. To serve, place bok choy in the centre of each plate and top with a fish fillet. Pour sauce around. Serve with rice.

DID YOU KNOW?
John Dory's thin profile front-on helps it sneak up on prey. Its large eyes at the front of its head give it bifocal vision — another helpful attribute in sizing up the whereabouts of the next meal.

Barbecued black bean salmon fillet on ginger and sesame vegetables

SERVES 4 | Recipe by Petra New

The sharpness of the black bean in this dish cuts through the creaminess of the salmon perfectly.

4 × 180g salmon fillets, skin on, pin-boned

2 tbsp black bean sauce

1cm piece fresh ginger, grated

2 cloves garlic, crushed

2 tbsp soy sauce

Salt and freshly ground pepper

GINGER AND SESAME VEGETABLES

1 courgette

1 carrot

½ red capsicum

½ yellow capsicum

1 bunch (200g) choy sum

2cm piece fresh ginger

1 spring onion

2 tbsp kecap manis

2 tbsp soy sauce

1 tsp sesame oil

Cooking spray

¼ cup white sesame seeds, toasted, for garnish

1. Score salmon twice on the skin side.

2. In a bowl mix together black bean sauce, ginger, garlic, soy sauce, salt and pepper. Rub over both sides of salmon and set aside.

3. To make ginger and sesame vegetables, slice courgette, carrot and capsicums into batons. Trim the choy sum. Slice ginger into matchsticks and thinly slice spring onion on the diagonal. Rinse all under cold water, shake off any excess, then toss together in a bowl.

4. Mix kecap manis, soy sauce and sesame oil in a bowl.

5. Oil the chargrill of the barbecue well. Over medium heat, chargrill salmon fillets for 3–5 minutes on each side – try not to move salmon for at least 3 minutes before turning to allow it to seal, making it easier to turn over without sticking.

6. Place a barbecue liner on the hot plate and lightly spray with cooking spray. Place vegetables all except ginger on the liner, then stir-fry for a few mintutes. Add ginger and continue to cook. Season to taste.

7. Organise the corners of the barbecue mat so that it can easily be removed from the barbecue by holding the four corners together, then pour over the sauce and continue to move the vegetables around until al dente.

8. Pick up the mat and pour all the vegetables and sauce onto a serving platter. Top with salmon and sprinkle with toasted sesame seeds.

Barbecued fish with hot and sour chilli sauce

SERVES 4 | Recipe by Petra New

The trick to knowing if your fish steak is cooked is to give the spine bone a little wiggle – if it comes away from the flesh, it is done.

HOT AND SOUR CHILLI SAUCE
Zest of 1 lime and juice of 3 limes
1 long red chilli, deseeded and sliced
1 tbsp grated dark palm sugar
2 tbsp fish sauce
¼ cup fresh basil leaves, chopped

2 cloves garlic, crushed
2 tbsp peanut oil
¼ cup chopped fresh coriander
4 × 180g fish steaks (e.g. hapuku, salmon or kingfish)
Salt and freshly ground pepper
4 cups steamed white rice, to serve

1. To make hot and sour chilli sauce, mix together ingredients (except basil) until palm sugar has dissolved, then add basil.

2. Mix together garlic, peanut oil and coriander and use to coat fish steaks. Season.

3. Chargrill fish steaks over medium–high heat until there is a good 5mm of cooked fish around the outside, then turn and cook on the other side.

4. To serve, use a mould to shape rice on your serving plate (or spoon on if you don't have a mould), top with a fish steak and pour over sauce.

Chargrilled fish fillets with balsamic mushrooms ▶

SERVES 4 AS A STARTER | Recipe by John Campbell

Kingfish is a great choice to match these full-flavoured mushrooms.

2 tbsp extra virgin olive oil, plus extra for drizzling
1 red onion, thinly sliced
2 cloves garlic, chopped
200g portobello mushrooms, sliced
1 tbsp chopped flat-leaf parsley
2 tsp chopped fresh thyme
Salt and New York cut pepper (see glossary page 276) or freshly ground pepper
1 tbsp balsamic reduction (available from specialty stores)
4 × 120g seasonal fish fillets (e.g. kingfish)

1. Pour oil onto a hot grill plate, then add the onion, garlic and mushrooms. Toss for 2–3 minutes.

2. Transfer mushroom mix to a bowl. Stir through herbs (reserving some for garnish) and seasoning, and add balsamic reduction.

3. Drizzle fish fillets with a little oil and barbecue on the hot grill for 2 minutes each side. Season to taste.

4. To serve, divide mushrooms between 4 plates and top with fish fillets and a sprinkle of herbs.

DID YOU KNOW?
The largest kingfish in the world are caught around New Zealand – up to 2.5 metres or 70 kilograms, as against the more usual 100 centimetres or 10–15 kilograms.

Barbecued chilli squid with Asian spices and green beans

SERVES 4 | Recipe by John Campbell

Asian flavours blend with the crunch of the beans and the soft texture of the chargrilled spiced squid to create this delicious salad.

SAUCE

60ml peanut oil

1 large onion, sliced

2 cloves garlic, crushed

2cm piece fresh ginger, chopped

1 tsp turmeric

1–2 chillies, seeds included, chopped

20g palm sugar

1 tbsp chopped fresh coriander

1 tbsp chopped fresh mint

2 tsp fish sauce

300ml chicken or fish stock (see recipe page 272) or water

Sea salt and freshly ground pepper

400g squid tubes, cleaned and sliced

200g green beans, blanched

100g blanched peanuts, roasted, to garnish

1. To make sauce, heat a pot over a medium–low heat and add one-third of the peanut oil and onion and garlic. Cook slowly for approximately 10 minutes to soften the onion, then add the remaining sauce ingredients (except for salt and pepper). Reduce liquid a little (to sauce consistency), then season to taste.

2. In a bowl, mix squid with half the remaining peanut oil, then season. Chargrill squid on the barbecue for 2–3 minutes, taking care not to overcook.

3. Toss the beans through the rest of the peanut oil. Cook on the barbecue for a few minutes, seasoning to taste.

4. To serve, place sauce in a bowl or platter and top with squid and beans. Sprinkle with peanuts.

Grilled fish fillets with chilli jam-spiced eggplant relish and green beans

SERVES 4 | Recipe by Marco Edwardes

A beautiful, simple dish. When it is in season, try asparagus in place of the green beans.

CHILLI JAM
(MAKES APPROXIMATELY 400ML)

1 tbsp olive oil

½ red onion, chopped

½ red capsicum, chopped

10 cherry tomatoes, cut in half

1 red chilli, deseeded and chopped

Zest and juice of 1 lemon

1 tbsp chopped fresh coriander
(root and leaves)

⅓ cup brown sugar

1 tbsp sambal oelek

1 tbsp fish sauce

Sea salt and freshly ground pepper

SPICED EGGPLANT RELISH

2 tbsp olive oil

2 cloves garlic, finely diced

2 shallots, finely sliced

2 tbsp capers, rinsed

4 anchovy fillets, chopped

3 tbsp chilli jam (see above)

2 tbsp red wine vinegar

4 tbsp chopped flat-leaf parsley

1 small eggplant, diced

4 × 160g fish fillets, skin on and boned

250g green beans (or asparagus)

Olive oil

Salt and freshly ground pepper

1 lemon, cut into wedges, for garnish

1. To make chilli jam, heat olive oil and fry onion and capsicum until soft. Add remaining ingredients and simmer for 30 minutes.

2. When cool, blend until smooth and adjust seasoning.

3. To make spiced eggplant relish, heat olive oil in a pot and fry garlic and shallots until golden.

4. Add capers, anchovies, prepared chilli jam, red wine vinegar, parsley and eggplant. Mix together. Cook for another 5 minutes over low heat until all flavours are well blended. Season to taste.

5. Rub fish fillets and green beans or asparagus with olive oil, salt and pepper.

6. Grill green beans or asparagus until al dente. Set aside until fish is cooked.

7. Cook fish in a little oil on a barbecue for 2 minutes skin-side down and then 1 minute on the other side (depending on thickness of fish).

8. To serve, divide eggplant relish among 4 dinner plates, arrange green beans or asparagus on the side and place grilled fish on top. Garnish with lemon wedges and serve immediately.

Mediterranean-style grilled scampi

SERVES 4 | Recipe by Mark Dronjak

Grilled scampi blended with citrus and olive oil makes a tasty meal. You can also use prawns in this dish.

24 scampi (or prawns), cut in half lengthwise
Juice of 1 lemon
2 sprigs oregano, leaves roughly chopped
3 tbsp roughly chopped flat-leaf parsley
Olive oil
Sea salt and freshly ground pepper
Handful of mesclun leaves
1 lemon, cut into wedges, to serve

1. Place scampi in a bowl with lemon juice, oregano, parsley and a good splash of olive oil. Season to taste.
2. Quickly cook scampi in a medium–hot frying pan, placing cut-side down first.
3. Serve with a few mesclun leaves, garnished with lemon wedges and accompanied by small forks or toothpicks for eating with.

DID YOU KNOW?
Researchers use deepwater digital photography to count scampi burrows in areas that have been fished. They have found this a reliable way to estimate scampi numbers for managing quotas.

Crispy tiger prawns with lime and chilli ▶

SERVES 4 | Recipe by Jo Cooper

Place some lemon slices into small finger bowls of water and have on hand – things will get messy.

16 large whole tiger prawns
1 clove garlic, chopped
1–2 Kaffir lime leaves, finely sliced
Flaky sea salt and cracked pepper
1 red chilli, deseeded (optional) and finely chopped
2 tbsp olive oil
4 grilled lime halves (see recipe page 271), to serve

1. Combine all ingredients (except limes) in a bowl and mix well.
2. Heat barbecue hot plate. Once hot, add prawns and grill until pink, turning once.
3. Serve prawns with grilled lime halves.

Whole barbecue-grilled market fish with Greek potato mash

SERVES 4 | Recipe by John Campbell

You can't go wrong with a whole barbecued fish. Great at the bach.

2 tsp cumin seeds

1 tsp garam masala

1 tsp Cajun spice mix (see recipe page 261)

Zest of 1 lemon

2 whole seasonal fish (500–700g each), gutted and scaled, fins trimmed

3 tbsp extra virgin olive oil

½ lemon, sliced

Salt and freshly ground pepper

Handful of fresh parsley, coriander and bay leaf

GREEK POTATO MASH

400g Agria potatoes, peeled and boiled until soft

50ml white wine vinegar

4–6 cloves garlic, crushed

150ml olive oil

Salt and freshly ground pepper

4 grilled lemon halves (see recipe page 271), to serve

1. Make a rub by combining spices and zest.

2. Make 2 cuts into flesh on both sides of fish and rub in spices. Drizzle with a little of the oil. Place lemon, salt, pepper and herbs into the cavity of each fish and stand for 20 minutes before cooking.

3. Heat up the barbecue, and when hot sprinkle with a little more of the oil. Place fish on the hot plate. Put the hood down and grill for 5–7 minutes. Turn fish and add a little more oil. Grill for a further 5–7 minutes, depending on the size of the fish. Check if cooked (the eyes should be white).

4. To make Greek potato mash, mash potatoes while warm and slowly add vinegar, garlic and oil. Season to taste.

5. Serve fish on a platter with a splash of olive oil, and grilled lemon halves and Greek potato mash on the side.

DID YOU KNOW?

All snapper begin life as females. During their third and fourth years of life, about half of them change sex, balancing the adult population evenly between male and female.

Chargrilled maple and apple salmon steaks, baked potatoes and fennel slaw

SERVES 4 | Recipe by Petra New

Fennel can be an overpowering flavour, so make sure you slice it thinly.

MARINADE
80ml maple syrup
125ml fresh apple juice
1 tbsp wholegrain mustard
1 tsp fennel seeds, dry-roasted

4 × 180–200g salmon steaks, pin-boned
4 medium potatoes, unpeeled
100g butter, softened
2 tbsp chopped chives
Salt and freshly ground pepper

DRESSING
2 tbsp mayonnaise
1 tbsp apple syrup
Juice of ½ lemon
Salt and freshly ground pepper

FENNEL SLAW
1 fennel bulb, thinly sliced
2 sweet apples, cored and julienned
½ stalk celery, thinly sliced
2 tbsp chopped flat-leaf parsley

1. To make marinade, mix together maple syrup, apple juice, mustard and fennel seeds. Pour marinade over salmon steaks and allow to marinate for 10 minutes.

2. Wash potatoes and place them in a pot. Cover with cold water, add a pinch of salt and bring to the boil. Simmer until a knife can easily pierce the skin, but they are still slightly firm. Drain.

3. Mix butter and chives together. Season to taste. Place on a piece of cling film and roll into a firm cylinder. Place in freezer to set.

4. When potatoes are well drained, pierce them a few times with a knife. Place each potato in a piece of tin foil and wrap and place on barbecue at a medium heat until fully cooked, turning often for even cooking.

5. Mix together dressing ingredients and season to taste. Gently mix dressing with fennel slaw ingredients until well combined.

6. Oil chargrill of the barbecue well, set to medium heat and place salmon on grill. Season to taste. When you have 10mm of cooked flesh, turn. Salmon is cooked when centre bone can easily be removed.

7. When potatoes are done, make a deep cross on the top of each, slightly squeeze and then place a slice of chive butter in the hole.

8. Serve salmon with slaw and a baked potato.

Ginger and manuka honey-glazed hot-smoked kahawai with avocado salsa

SERVES 4 | Recipe by Steve Roberts

A simple hot-smoked fish recipe incorporating ginger and the unique flavour of manuka honey.

SMOKE MIX

Manuka sawdust

3 tbsp brown sugar

1 star anise

1 cinnamon stick

2–3 cardamom pods

1 vanilla pod

Peel of 1 orange

AVOCADO SALSA

2 avocados, flesh roughly chopped

1 red capsicum, finely diced

½ red onion, finely sliced

Handful of flat-leaf parsley, chopped

Squeeze of lemon juice

Salt and freshly ground pepper

4 × 170g kahawai fillets (or salmon or
   trevally, or two whole fish butterflied,
   scaled and skin on)

Pinch of flaky sea salt

3–4 tsp brown sugar

2–3 tbsp manuka honey

3–4 tbsp ginger beer cordial concentrate

Squeeze of lemon juice

Pinch of ground ginger

Pinch of white pepper

50ml avocado oil

4 thick slices ciabatta

1. To make smoke mix, mix together all ingredients and place in a smoker lined with tin foil.

2. To make avocado salsa, mix all ingredients well.

3. Rub kahawai fillets with sea salt and brown sugar. Leave for 5–10 minutes. Brush off excess salt and sugar mix and place on a pre-greased wire rack ready for smoking.

4. Combine manuka honey, ginger beer concentrate, lemon juice and ground ginger. Mix well. Brush onto fish. Sprinkle with white pepper.

5. Once the chips in the smoker start to smoke, put fish into smoker, turn heat to low (so the chips do not catch fire) and close lid. Fish will be ready in 10–15 minutes, depending on thickness. Check periodically to ensure an even smoke and adjust heat as needed – if smoke is too hot, it will give a bitter finish to the dish. This smoking process can also be applied to wok smoking or smoking on a barbecue.

6. Place smoked kahawai on a serving plate and drizzle with a little avocado oil.

7. Drizzle ciabatta with avocado oil and season. Grill ciabatta on a barbecue grill on low heat until golden.

8. To serve, top ciabatta with avocado salsa and some smoked kahawai.

Orange and sage barbecued mussels

SERVES 4 | Recipe by Petra New

Use a barbecue liner to capture all the juices in this dish – plus it will keep the barbecue clean.

Extra virgin olive oil
½ red onion, sliced
2 cloves garlic
1kg mussels, cleaned
Zest and segments of 1 orange
1 tbsp chopped fresh sage leaves
1 tbsp wholegrain mustard
300ml fresh orange juice
Salt and freshly ground pepper
2 tbsp chopped flat-leaf parsley,
    for garnish

1. Place a barbecue liner on the hot plate of the barbecue on low heat. Lightly drizzle liner with oil, then sauté onion and garlic until translucent.

2. Add mussels, turn up the heat a little and add orange zest, sage and wholegrain mustard over mussels.

3. Turn up the heat to high, pour over orange juice, and season to taste. Stir again. (The heat of the barbecue will sizzle and thicken the liquid and stop it pouring off.) Close the hood and cook for a few minutes, until mussels are open.

4. Lift up the corners of the barbecue liner to remove the mussels. Pour onto a serving platter, including sauce. Garnish with flat-leaf parsley and orange segments.

Grilled prawns with tomato, feta and dill ▶

SERVES 4 | Recipe by John Campbell

The chilli provides a nice little kick.

500g fresh tomatoes
50ml extra virgin olive oil
500g raw prawns, shelled
2 tsp butter
1 small onion, diced
2 cloves garlic, chopped
½ red chilli, deseeded (optional) and chopped
100ml white wine
1 tbsp chopped fresh dill
200g feta, crumbled
Salt and freshly ground pepper
100g panko breadcrumbs

1. Preheat oven to grill 220°C.

2. Prepare tomatoes by criss-crossing the bottom of each tomato with a small, sharp knife and removing the eye. Place into a pot of boiling water for 1 minute. Refresh in cold water. When cool, peel skins off and discard, then cut tomatoes into quarters, remove seeds and finely dice.

3. Heat a sauté pan, add half the oil and cook prawns in batches until pink. Remove.

4. In the same pan, heat butter and cook onion, garlic and chilli until onion is translucent, without colouring. Add wine and reduce until nearly dry. Add tomatoes, cook for a few minutes or until thick. Add prawns, dill and feta. Season to taste. Place on a suitable platter or into bowls.

5. Top with breadcrumbs, drizzle with remaining oil and place under the grill until golden.

Grilled crayfish

SERVES 4 AS A STARTER | Recipe by Jo Cooper and Petra New

Whenever crayfish is at hand, it's a toss-up between poached crayfish with fresh mayonnaise or this recipe. Either one goes down very well with a glass of chilled wine while sitting outside with friends.

1 live crayfish

2 tbsp olive oil

50g butter, melted

Sea salt and cracked black pepper

2 tbsp chopped flat-leaf parsley

4 grilled lemon halves (see recipe page 271), to serve

1. Dispatch crayfish (see methods page 11).

2. Cut through the middle of the crayfish (lengthwise), holding down with a cloth. Remove digestive tract and guts from the head (unless a preferred flavour).

3. Heat barbecue.

4. Mix olive oil and half the butter together and brush crayfish flesh with it. Season to taste.

5. Place crayfish flesh-side down on the barbecue grill for 2–3 minutes, depending on size of the crayfish – longer if the crayfish is large. Turn over. Cook a further 2–3 minutes. The crayfish is cooked when the flesh becomes firmer and can pull away from the shell (which will turn a bright orange colour).

6. Brush flesh with remaining butter and sprinkle with chopped parsley. Serve with grilled lemon halves.

Barbecued sticky Chinese orange and ginger snapper parcels

SERVES 4 | Recipe by Petra New

The success of this recipe relies upon making sure the glaze is really thick, as the steam from the parcel dilutes the glaze during cooking.

300ml orange juice

3 tbsp kecap manis

1cm piece fresh ginger, grated

1 clove garlic, crushed

1 star anise

½ tsp Chinese five spice

1 tbsp chopped fresh coriander

1 courgette, cut into batons

1 carrot, cut into batons

½ yellow capsicum, cut into batons

4 × 180g snapper fillets, skin on

Salt and freshly ground pepper

1. Combine orange juice, kecap manis, ginger, garlic, star anise and Chinese five spice in a small pot and simmer over a high heat until it has reduced by half. When reduced, add chopped coriander and allow to cool.

2. Lay out four pieces of tin foil (each approximately 30cm square) and line each with a smaller piece of baking paper.

3. Mix together prepared courgette, carrot and capsicum. Place a quarter of the mix in the middle of each piece of paper.

4. Score the thicker part of snapper fillets on the skin side – this will allow for even cooking and for flavours to penetrate.

5. Place fish on top of vegetables and season with salt and pepper. Spoon orange sauce over the fish.

6. Wrap each parcel, bringing together two sides of the foil and folding. Repeat, making a double fold, then fold over the other ends twice as well to ensure neither the steam nor the cooking juices escape.

7. Place parcels on the hot plate of a medium–hot barbecue and cook with the hood down for 4–6 minutes, depending on thickness of fillet.

8. To serve, carefully open each parcel, pushing the sides away to expose contents.

Barbecued bluenose on crushed potatoes with caper, lemon and olive dressing

SERVES 4 | Recipe by Mark Dronjak

The dressing is just ideal with the fish and crushed potatoes.

4 x 150g fresh bluenose fillets (or use porae, tarakihi, lemonfish or ling)

Olive oil for drizzling

Sea salt and cracked white pepper

400g small potatoes, skin on

4 tbsp finely chopped flat-leaf parsley

CAPER, LEMON AND OLIVE DRESSING

75g capers, roughly chopped

Juice of 2 lemons

75g pitted green olives, finely chopped

75g pitted Kalamata olives, finely chopped

4 tbsp roughly chopped flat-leaf parsley

50ml lemon-infused olive oil

2 tbsp olive oil

1. Drizzle bluenose with a little olive oil and season to taste.

2. Cook potatoes, then drain and crush, adding parsley, a little olive oil and seasoning.

3. To make caper, lemon and olive dressing, combine capers, lemon juice, olives, parsley and olive oils in a small saucepan and heat slightly (do not overheat – warm only). Adjust seasoning.

4. Place fish fillets on a hot barbecue flat plate and cook, turning after a few minutes and allowing to colour.

5. Divide crushed potatoes between four plates, stack fish on top and serve with dressing spooned over.

DID YOU KNOW?
Despite their rapid growth as young fish, porae are quite long-lived – large fish may be up to 30 years old.

Bruschetta with seared octopus

SERVES 4 | Recipe by Mark Dronjak

A great starter for a Mediterranean-style barbecue.

300g baby octopus
2 tbsp finely chopped fresh oregano
3 cloves garlic (2 finely chopped and 1 whole
    for rubbing)
Juice of 1 lemon
Olive oil
Sea salt and freshly ground pepper
3 medium–large vine-ripened tomatoes
8 fresh basil leaves, roughly chopped
8 thin–medium slices ciabatta bread

1. Place baby octopus in a bowl with oregano,
   finely chopped garlic, lemon juice, a good
   lug of olive oil and seasoning. Leave
   to marinate.

2. Dice tomatoes and place in a bowl. Add basil
   leaves and season. Add some olive oil and
   mix through.

3. Heat a grill plate until hot. Drizzle bread
   with a little olive oil and toast on the grill
   plate until lightly coloured and scored.
   Remove and rub with whole garlic clove.
   Drizzle with a little more oil.

4. Add octopus to hot grill and sear quickly
   and evenly.

5. To serve, divide half of the tomato mix
   between bread slices. Season to taste. Place
   octopus on bruschetta, completing the
   dish by arranging remaining tomato over
   and around.

Grilled flounder ▶

SERVES 4 | Recipe by John Campbell

'No fuss flounder' makes a great weekend brunch.

100g butter, softened
100ml olive oil
4 flounder (about 500g)
Plain flour, for dusting
25g Cajun spice mix (see recipe page 261)
4 tbsp Worcestershire sauce
4 grilled lemon halves (see recipe page 271), to serve
Hot buttered toast, to serve

1. Preheat oven to grill 250°C and turn on the
   warming drawer of the oven. You will only
   fit two flounders on a tray, so heat up two
   lipped trays with a little of the oil and butter.

2. Dust each flounder with flour. Combine
   remaining butter and oil. Dip the black
   skin-side of each fish into this mixture.
   Place 2 fish on each tray with the black skin
   facing up. Sprinkle with Cajun spice mix
   and Worcestershire sauce and place one tray
   under the grill for 12–15 minutes.

3. Remove tray and transfer to the warming
   drawer. Place second tray of flounder under
   the grill for 12–15 minutes. When this is
   ready, put it in the warming drawer and
   briefly grill the first tray of flounder to
   warm it through.

4. Serve flounder on large plates and pour over
   cooking juices. Serve half a grilled lemon with
   each flounder and accompany with plenty of
   hot buttered toast.

Ultimate seafood mixed grill

SERVES 4 | Recipe by Steve Roberts

There's a little of everything here – and it's oh-so-easy to put together.

MOROCCAN SPICE

1 tsp each coriander and cumin seeds

2 tsp cardamom seeds

¼ cinnamon stick

8 cloves

2½ tsp paprika

2 tsp garlic powder

Salt and freshly ground pepper

CITRUS MAYONNAISE

2 egg yolks

2 tsp citrus juice

1 tsp water

1 tsp Dijon mustard

½ tsp brown sugar

300ml grapeseed oil

Salt and freshly ground pepper

400g salmon fillet, skinned, boned, cubed

16 raw prawn cutlets

1 lemon and 1 lime, each cut into wedges

2 chorizo sausages

2 large tomatoes, vine if available

1 tbsp olive oil, for drizzling

Handful each of fresh basil and Italian
    parsley, chopped

4 small or 2 large field mushrooms

4 thick slices ciabatta

1 clove garlic

12 slices streaky bacon

4 eggs

1. Place 8 wooden skewers in water to soak.

2. To make Moroccan spice, toast coriander, cumin and cardamom seeds, cinnamon and cloves in a hot, dry pan, then grind using a mortar and pestle. Add paprika, garlic powder and seasoning to taste.

3. To make citrus mayonnaise, combine all ingredients except the oil in a bowl with a little seasoning. Sit the bowl on a damp cloth and slowly start whisking in oil, being careful not to add too much at once. Adjust seasoning and refrigerate until ready to use.

4. Thread salmon cubes onto 4 skewers. Using 4 separate skewers, thread 4 prawns on each, alternating them with a wedge of lemon or lime. Season to taste.

5. Cut chorizo sausages in half lengthwise and score.

6. Cut tomatoes in half, drizzle with olive oil, dust with chopped herbs and season. Drizzle mushrooms with a little oil and season.

7. Drizzle ciabatta with olive oil. On a moderately hot barbecue, grill ciabatta to a golden brown. Remove and let cool slightly, rub with fresh garlic and set aside.

8. Rub salmon with Moroccan spice and leave to marinate for 5 minutes. Place on pre-oiled grill and cook to medium rare. Remove and cover with foil to keep warm.

9. Add prawn and citrus skewers to the barbecue, along with chorizo, bacon, tomatoes and mushrooms. While these are cooking, gently poach the eggs. Remove food from barbecue.

10. Serve mixed grill with citrus mayonnaise.

Kasbah mussels with tomatoes, coriander, olives and capsicum

SERVES 4 | Recipe by Mark Dronjak

North African spices resulting in a hint of Morocco.

Olive oil for frying

1 red capsicum, finely diced

1 green capsicum, finely diced

2 cloves garlic, roughly chopped

½ cup Kalamata olives

½ tsp ground coriander

½ tsp turmeric

1 tsp paprika

½ tsp ground cumin

¼ tsp ground cinnamon

½ tsp ground ginger

Pinch of ground cloves

Pinch of chilli powder

Pinch of white sugar

½ cup crushed tomatoes

Zest and juice of 1 lemon

Flaky sea salt

24 mussels, blanched and in the half shell, foot and beard removed

Handful of parsley, chopped, for garnish

2 lemons, cut into wedges, to serve

1. Preheat oven to grill 200°C.

2. Heat a good splash of olive oil in a pan. Add capsicum, garlic, olives, spices and sugar. Stir over a medium heat. Add crushed tomatoes and a little water to mix, if required. Add lemon zest and juice. Adjust seasoning to taste.

3. Place half-shell mussels on a baking tray and spoon over sauce.

4. Grill until heated through (approximately 10 minutes).

5. Serve mussels on a platter, garnished with chopped parsley and lemon wedges.

Hot-smoked salmon with potato cakes and beurre blanc

SERVES 4 | Recipe by John Campbell

A quick smoked seafood technique that can be done in the oven, on a hooded barbecue or in a traditional smoker. Lime or lemon glaze (see page 264) can be used in place of beurre blanc.

Splash each of olive oil and soy sauce

400g fresh salmon (or trout if available), skin on, pin-boned

Sprinkle each of brown sugar, cumin seeds, paprika, Cajun spice mix (see recipe page 261), caraway seeds , fennel seeds, yellow and brown mustard seeds, freshly ground pepper, sea salt

100g manuka wood chips, for smoking

BEURRE BLANC

500ml fish stock (see recipe page 272)

100ml dry white wine

2 tbsp white vinegar

1 small onion, sliced

2 bay leaves

Few parsley stalks

Few sprigs of thyme

10 whole peppercorns

250ml cream

185g cold, unsalted butter, cut into cubes

White pepper

POTATO CAKES

400g cooked Agria potatoes, skin on

1 tbsp chopped fresh chives

Salt and freshly ground pepper

Plain flour, for moulding

1. Brush olive oil and soy over the salmon, then sprinkle over other ingredients (except wood chips). Stand for 30 minutes. Place salmon on a greased oven tray.

2. Preheat oven to 230°C. Do not use fanbake.

3. Place wood chips in an old pan and heat on stovetop until smoking, then place in the bottom of the oven (not on a rack) and turn on the extractor in your kitchen.

4. Place salmon in the middle of the oven and leave to smoke for 5–8 minutes. Allow to rest, to serve warm or at room temperature.

5. To make beurre blanc, put stock, wine, vinegar, onion, herbs and peppercorns in a pot. Bring to the boil and slowly reduce the liquid by two-thirds.

6. Add cream and reduce by half. Remove from the heat and strain.

7. Add butter, two or three cubes at a time, whisking to combine into sauce. Don't re-boil or sauce will split – just keep warm until required. Taste and season with white pepper.

8. To make potato cakes, peel off skin and grate the potato. Mix in the chives and seasoning and mould with a little flour to form 4 even-sized small discs. Pan-fry or barbecue until golden.

9. To serve, place a potato cake on each plate, top with a piece of salmon and spoon over a little of the beurre blanc.

Fish burgers

SERVES 4 | Recipe by Colin Doyle

Fresh grilled fish fillets are the star in these burgers, which combine peppery rocket with a rich garlic aioli and crunchy pickled onions. Serve with some potato wedges for a nice twist on fish and chips.

1 medium red onion

½ tsp salt

½ tsp ground sumac (optional)

1 tsp lemon juice

AIOLI

2 cloves garlic

Salt

1 egg yolk

1 tsp Dijon mustard

100ml light olive oil

1 tbsp lemon juice

2 tbsp capers, finely chopped

4 fresh ciabatta buns

Salt and freshly ground pepper

4 × 120g white fish fillets (e.g. gurnard, tarakihi, snapper or hoki)

100g baby rocket

1 ripe tomato, sliced

1. Thinly slice red onion and place in a non-reactive bowl. Sprinkle with salt, sumac (if using) and lemon juice. Set aside until ready to assemble burgers.

2. Preheat oven to grill 220°C.

3. Prepare aioli by crushing garlic with a little salt using a mortar and pestle or in a food processor. Transfer garlic purée to a small bowl. Add egg yolk and mustard and beat with a whisk until pale and frothy. Slowly add olive oil, at the beginning drop by drop, not adding more until the previous addition is fully incorporated. When all the oil is added and aioli is thick, mix in lemon juice and chopped capers.

4. Slice buns and place under the grill for a few minutes to lightly toast.

5. Season fish fillets and grill or fry over medium heat for 3 minutes per side or until done (depending on thickness of fillet).

6. To serve, spread a little aioli on each half of the toasted buns and then assemble the burger with rocket, a slice of tomato, fish fillet and a pile of onions.

DID YOU KNOW?

Hoki's easy-flaking and mild-tasting flesh makes it particularly suitable for popular fast-food products like fish fingers and fish burgers.

Pan-seared, deep-fried
and sautéed

Herb and panko crumbed fish fillets   166

Prosciutto-wrapped medallions of salmon with scallop and herb mousse   168

Wok-fried prawns with lemongrass and tamarind   170

Salt and pepper squid with sweet chilli and wasabi aioli   171

Seared monkfish fillets with semi-dried tomatoes and fresh herbs   172

Seared tuna Niçoise   174

Whole pan-seared flounder   174

Tempura of prawn   176

Seared snapper on potato and green bean salad with watercress pesto   177

Fennel-crusted kingfish with olive oil-crushed potatoes   178

Moroccan fish with almond couscous   180

Pan-seared John Dory with creamy roasted capsicums and refried beans   182

Crispy-skinned snapper with mushrooms, ginger and tropical fruit salsa   183

Snapper with green pea purée and crispy shrimp polenta   184

Balinese fried fish   186

Beer-battered fish fillets   186

Mixed seafood and vegetable stir-fry with cashew nuts   188

Bacon-wrapped salmon on portobello mushrooms   189

Pan-fried hapuku with sautéed potatoes   190

Seared tuna rolls with seaweed salad   192

Sweet and sour wok-fried crab   193

Crispy-skinned snapper with red capsicum and fennel confit and black olive tapenade   194

Market fish with butterbean purée, scallops and chorizo with salsa verde   196

Snapper on curry-spiced cauliflower florets with coconut cream and lychee foam   198

Eggs Benedict with salmon on kumara cakes and orange Hollandaise   199

Pan-fried broadbill in a saffron sauce   200

Herb and panko crumbed fish fillets

SERVES 4 | Recipe by Colin Doyle

If you crumb the fillets about 20 minutes ahead of time and place them in the fridge wrapped in cling film, you will get better adhesion. Make sure the oil is very hot before the fish is added to the pan, to stop the crumb from absorbing too much oil.

1 bunch parsley, finely chopped

2 sprigs fresh mint, finely chopped

6 fresh sage leaves, finely chopped

2 cups panko breadcrumbs

2 eggs

½ cup milk

150g plain flour

1 tsp salt

4 × 160g fish fillets (any fresh white fish fillet is suitable), skin off

2 tbsp vegetable oil

4 grilled lemon halves (see recipe page 271), to serve

A few fried sage leaves, for garnish

1. Place herbs in a wide shallow bowl with panko crumbs.

2. Lightly beat eggs and milk in a separate wide, shallow bowl and set aside.

3. Season flour and place on a plate.

4. To crumb fish, lightly dust fillets with seasoned flour, shaking off the excess. Dip fillets in egg mix, and then finally into herb and crumb mix. It works best if you keep one hand for handling the fish and the other hand for gently pressing crumbs onto the fillets.

5. To fry fillets, heat a non-stick pan over medium heat and when hot, add oil. Fry fillets, taking care not to crowd the pan – it is far better to cook them in a couple of batches. Cook for approximately 4 minutes, or until crumb has developed a golden colour, before turning. Remove from pan and place on greaseproof paper.

6. Serve with grilled lemon halves and garnish with sage leaves.

Prosciutto-wrapped medallions of salmon with scallop and herb mousse

SERVES 4 | Recipe by Steve Roberts

A dish that requires a little bit of work, but is well worth the effort.

SCALLOP AND HERB MOUSSE

200g scallops

2 egg whites

Handful of chopped fresh basil

Handful of chopped fresh flat-leaf parsley

Salt and freshly ground pepper

400g salmon fillet, skinned and boned

8 slices prosciutto

Oil, for frying

Salt and freshly ground pepper

1 tbsp capers, rinsed

Juice of ½ lemon

1 medium fennel bulb, thinly sliced

Handful of baby watercress

CITRUS AND BLACK PEPPER DRESSING

150ml olive oil

50ml fresh orange juice

50ml fresh lemon juice

Pinch of caster sugar

1 tbsp freshly ground pepper

1. To make scallop and herb mousse, process scallops, egg whites, herbs and salt and pepper in a blender until a smooth consistency is reached. Sauté a little to check seasoning and adjust if necessary.

2. Split salmon fillet in half lengthwise. Pipe scallop mousse onto one half of salmon, place other half of fillet on top to create a sandwich. Wrap tightly in prosciutto and then in cling film. Chill for 30 minutes.

3. Preheat oven to 180°C.

4. Remove salmon from cling film. Heat a little oil in a sauté pan until hot. Season salmon and fry in pan until browned all over. Finish in oven for around 5–7 minutes. Remove from oven and rest for 5 minutes.

5. Add capers to pan and squeeze over lemon juice.

6. To make citrus and black pepper dressing, mix together all ingredients.

7. Slice salmon into 8 thin pieces on the bias, allowing 2 slices per portion, and arrange on plate. Place capers, fennel and cress in a mixing bowl and toss with dressing, reserving some for drizzling on the plate. Arrange on serving plates next to salmon with a drizzle of dressing.

Wok-fried prawns with lemongrass and tamarind

SERVES 4 | Recipe by Petra New

The flavours of lemongrass and tamarind in this dish will work well with crayfish or scampi, too.

3 tbsp canola oil

16 whole prawns, shell on (or scampi or crayfish)

3 red shallots, finely chopped

4 cloves garlic, crushed

1cm piece fresh ginger, grated

5cm length lemongrass, bruised and finely chopped

4 Kaffir lime leaves, torn into quarters

1 long green chilli, deseeded and sliced

2 tbsp tamarind pulp

2 tbsp soy sauce

2 tbsp fish sauce

2 tbsp grated palm sugar

½ cup water

1 tsp white pepper

½ cup Thai basil leaves

Juice of 1 lime

Fresh coriander leaves, for garnish

1. Heat wok to medium–high, add half the oil and stir-fry prawns for 3 minutes until they turn a bright orange/pink colour. Remove and set aside.

2. Add remaining oil and stir-fry shallots, garlic, ginger, lemongrass, Kaffir lime leaves and chilli. When shallots become translucent, add tamarind pulp, soy sauce, fish sauce, palm sugar and water. Bring to the boil.

3. Return prawns to the wok and season with white pepper.

4. Remove wok from the heat and toss through Thai basil leaves and lime juice.

5. To serve, arrange prawns into a high pile on a serving platter, pour over sauce and garnish with coriander leaves. Serve with a bowl of warm water to use as a finger bowl.

Salt and pepper squid with sweet chilli and wasabi aioli

SERVES 4 | Recipe by Mark Dronjak

You've got to love crispy and salty squid served with a creamy, lightly spiced dip.

SWEET CHILLI AND WASABI AIOLI

2 tbsp Thai sweet chilli sauce (vary according to taste and desired heat)

2 tsp wasabi paste (vary according to taste and desired heat)

Juice of ½ lemon

1 egg yolk

1 tsp creamy mustard

150–200ml sunflower or good-quality vegetable oil

Salt and freshly ground pepper

600g squid tubes

⅓ cup mixed Szechuan and white peppercorns, cracked

Sea salt

Olive oil

8 cherry tomatoes, for garnish

1 lemon, cut into wedges, to serve

Sprigs of flat-leaf parsley, for garnish

1. To make sweet chilli and wasabi aioli, combine all ingredients except the oil and seasoning in a very clean bowl. Drizzle oil in very slowly while mixing. Season to taste.

2. Prepare squid tubes by cutting each tube in half and scoring the inside flesh with a small sharp knife. Cut into pieces measuring 75–100mm wide.

3. Combine cracked pepper mix in a bowl with a good sprinkle of sea salt and a good splash of olive oil. Add squid. Toss and set aside to marinate for 15–30 minutes.

4. Cook squid in a hot pan until it starts to colour. Do not overcook, otherwise it can toughen.

5. Serve squid topped with some of the aioli and garnish with a few cherry tomatoes, lemon wedges and parsley sprigs. Serve remaining aioli in a side dish.

Seared monkfish fillets with semi-dried tomatoes and fresh herbs

SERVES 4 | Recipe by Mark Dronjak

A great combination of exceptional flavours; the sauce doubles as a colourful garnish.

Olive oil

2 cloves garlic, peeled and sliced

8 anchovy fillets, roughly chopped

100g semi-dried tomatoes, finely sliced

6 tbsp each chopped fresh basil, thyme and flat-leaf parsley

100ml dry white wine

Juice of 1 lemon

4 × 120g fresh monkfish fillets (or gurnard), skin on

200g cannellini beans, pre-cooked (canned are ideal) and drained

25g butter

100g Parmesan, grated

Sea salt and freshly ground pepper

50g fresh rocket leaves

1 lemon, cut into wedges, to serve

1. Preheat oven to 200°C.

2. Prepare sauce by heating a little olive oil in a pan. Add garlic, anchovies and tomatoes. Add chopped herbs. Splash with wine to highlight the flavour and add a good lug of olive oil and a squeeze of lemon juice.

3. Place monkfish fillets on a greased baking tray and bake for 10–15 minutes or until just cooked.

4. Ensure cannellini beans are well drained. Add a splash of olive oil and butter to a hot pan. Toss beans, taking care not to break them up. Add Parmesan and toss to combine well. Cook beans until just coloured and season to taste.

5. Serve monkfish on top of beans with sauce poured over. Finish with rocket leaves on the side and lemon wedges.

DID YOU KNOW?

The monkfish or stargazer is an expert at ambush. It lies almost completely concealed in its sandy burrow with its upward-looking eyes on the watch, then rushes its prey and grabs it with its capacious vertical mouth.

Seared tuna Niçoise

SERVES 4 | Recipe by John Campbell

Ensure the tuna is seared quickly and cooked just medium–rare to enjoy the full flavour of this amazing fish.

SALAD

150g small new potatoes, cooked, cooled and halved

150g green beans, trimmed, blanched and refreshed

1 red onion, finely sliced

3 medium vine-ripened tomatoes, cut into wedges

15 good-quality black olives, pitted and halved

6 anchovy fillets, diced (optional)

2 hard-boiled eggs, shelled and quartered

200ml balsamic dressing (see page 262 for basic vinaigrette and replace the white vinegar with balsamic vinegar)

Salt and freshly ground pepper

4 × 150g tuna steaks

Oil for frying

Fresh basil and chervil, for garnish

1. Place all salad ingredients in a mixing bowl and add enough dressing to just moisten. Season to taste.

2. Season tuna then sear in a little oil until medium–rare (about 1 minute on each side).

3. To serve, place tuna on top of salad divided among 4 plates and garnish with fresh basil and chervil.

Whole pan-seared flounder ▶

SERVES 2 | Recipe by Jo Cooper and Harrison McIntyre

A simple flounder recipe complemented with citrus and butter. Delicious for breakfast served with fresh white buttered bread.

3 tbsp plain flour

Salt and freshly ground pepper

1 fresh flounder, scaled, gutted and cleaned

1½ tbsp olive oil

20g butter

Juice of ½ lemon and ½ orange

2 tbsp chopped flat-leaf parsley

2 grilled lemon halves (see recipe page 271), to serve

1. Season flour and use it to lightly dust flounder.

2. Add oil to a hot frying pan. Place in flounder. Quickly fry on both sides until golden brown. Remove flounder and keep warm.

3. Add butter to the pan and allow it to froth, without browning. Add citrus juices, reduce slightly and then place flounder back into the warm pan.

4. Spoon citrus juices over flounder, sprinkle with parsley and serve with grilled lemon halves.

DID YOU KNOW?

'Right-eyed' flounders have an eye on each side of their head when they're larvae. As they grow, their left eye shifts to the right side of their head and the body's left side becomes their flat underside. 'Left-eyed' flounders start the same and go vice versa.

Tempura of prawn

SERVES 4 | Recipe by Steve Roberts

The lightness of the tempura batter allows the prawn to remain the main act.

TEMPURA DIPPING SAUCE

310ml dashi (instant)

60ml mirin

80ml Kikkoman soy sauce

24 large prawn cutlets, shelled and
   deveined, tail on

TEMPURA BATTER

125g cornflour

125g plain flour

1 tsp baking powder

2 tsp salt

2 tbsp canola oil

200ml soda water

Approximately 200ml ice-cold water

⅓ cup plain flour for dusting

4 grilled lime halves (see recipe page 271),
   to serve

1. To make tempura dipping sauce, combine all ingredients in a pot and bring to the boil. Remove from heat.

2. Make 3 cuts in the underbelly of each prawn, turn prawn over and push lightly on a hard surface – this will help stop them curling too much when cooked.

3. To make tempura batter, mix together cornflour, flour, baking powder, salt and oil. Add soda water and ice-cold water and mix. The finished batter should be a little lumpy.

4. Heat a deep-fryer to 175–180°C.

5. Dust prawns in flour. Holding them by the tail, dip them into batter then deep-fry in batches.

6. Serve immediately with tempura dipping sauce and grilled limes on the side.

Seared snapper on potato and green bean salad with watercress pesto

SERVES 4 | Recipe by Mark Dronjak

This salad perfectly complements the pesto and snapper.

WATERCRESS PESTO

1 clove garlic

½ cup pine nuts

Large handful of watercress leaves

Juice of 1–2 lemons

Olive oil

Sea salt and freshly ground pepper

200g small boiling potatoes, skin on

Olive oil

4 × 160g snapper fillets

120g fresh green beans (frozen whole baby beans are also ideal)

1. To make watercress pesto, combine garlic, pine nuts, watercress and lemon juice in a food processor. Add a good lug of olive oil and process until a smooth consistency with little flecks of nuts in it. Adjust seasoning to taste. Add more oil or lemon juice as desired for consistency and taste.

2. Cook potatoes in a pot of water until just done – a little firm is ideal.

3. Splash a little olive oil over snapper fillets and place in a hot pan. Sear and colour for a few minutes each side.

4. While snapper is cooking, blanch beans in a little salted water (if you time it right you can add beans to the same pot as the potatoes). Do not overcook – al dente is ideal.

5. Slice, quarter or cut potatoes into wedges, depending on size, and place in a bowl. Add beans and a spoon of pesto to add colour. Toss in a little olive oil and season.

6. Serve snapper on top of the warm salad with a good spoonful of pesto over the fish.

Fennel-crusted kingfish with olive oil-crushed potatoes

SERVES 4 | Recipe by Steve Roberts

Fennel is a great friend to seafood. This is a full-of-flavour Mediterranean-inspired recipe.

FENNEL SPICE MIX
100g fennel seeds
30g black peppercorns
15g sea salt

TOMATO AND BASIL DRESSING
1 red capsicum, deseeded and finely diced
2 large tomatoes, deseeded and diced
Handful of fresh basil leaves, finely sliced
200ml olive oil
Salt and freshly ground pepper
Pinch of sugar (optional)

400g gourmet baby potatoes
Salt
100ml olive oil
10 pitted black olives, chopped
Handful of fresh flat-leaf parsley and basil, chopped
Salt and freshly ground pepper
4 × 120g kingfish fillets, skinned and boned (or tuna or broadbill)
Oil for cooking
200g spinach

1. To make fennel spice mix, place all ingredients in a pan and gently heat until fragrant. Cool and then grind mix using a pestle and mortar.

2. To make tomato and basil dressing, combine all ingredients and season to taste. If you find it a little sharp, add a pinch of sugar.

3. Place potatoes in a pot of cold water with a little salt and boil until soft. Drain well. Crush lightly and stir through olive oil, olives and herbs. Season to taste.

4. Sprinkle both sides of kingfish with fennel spice mix. Sear in a hot pan in a little oil for approximately 1 minute on each side, depending on thickness. Kingfish should be served medium–rare.

5. Wash spinach and then lightly wilt in a sauté pan.

6. To serve, place some potato in the centre of each serving plate, top with kingfish and spinach and drizzle dressing around the plate.

Moroccan fish with almond couscous

SERVES 4 | Recipe by Marco Edwardes

A favourite winter warmer that is best with hapuku, bluenose or kingfish.

600g fish fillets, cut into bite-sized pieces
3 cloves garlic, crushed
2 tsp grated fresh ginger
3 tsp Moroccan spice mix
2 tsp smoked paprika
2 tsp freshly ground pepper
½ cup olive oil

ALMOND COUSCOUS

2 cups couscous
2 tsp raisins
50g slivered almonds
¼ tsp ground cinnamon
2 tsp sliced spring onions
¼ cup extra virgin olive oil
2 cups chicken stock, warmed

Olive oil
1 large onion, finely diced
1 large carrot, finely diced
2 stalks celery, finely diced
1 cup pitted black olives, sliced
2 tsp preserved lemon skin (see recipe
    page 271), finely chopped
1 tsp anchovies, thinly sliced
1 cup dates, pitted and chopped
1 cup tomato purée
⅓ cup chopped mixed fresh mint
    and parsley

1. Place fish in a bowl and add garlic, ginger, Moroccan spice mix, paprika, pepper and olive oil. Stir until fish is well coated and set aside.

2. While fish is marinating, to make almond couscous, place couscous in a bowl and add raisins, almonds, cinnamon, spring onions and oil. Stir until well combined. Pour warm chicken stock over couscous until just covered, then cover with cling film and set aside to cook.

3. Preheat a large frying pan on high and add a small amount of olive oil. Add onion, carrot and celery and stir gently.

4. Move vegetables to the outside of the pan and place marinated fish in the centre. Seal fish pieces then stir to combine fish and vegetables. Reduce heat to medium.

5. Add olives, preserved lemon skin, anchovies and dates. Add tomato purée and stir for a few more minutes.

6. Serve Moroccan fish garnished with mint and parsley with almond couscous on the side.

Pan-seared John Dory with creamy roasted capsicums and refried beans

SERVES 4 | Recipe by Colin Doyle

This is a very homely dish, so you won't find it in many restaurants. It combines slow-cooked strips of capsicum (rajas) with cream and garlic, which perfectly complements a nice piece of John Dory.

1 red capsicum

1 green capsicum (alternatively use a fresh poblano chilli, if available)

1 medium onion

Oil for frying

2 cloves garlic, minced

1 pickled jalapeño chilli, minced

1½ cups cream

Pinch of dried Mexican oregano (available from specialty stores)

100g pancetta, finely diced

440g can black beans (or pinto beans)

Pinch of epazote (available from specialty stores, optional)

⅓ cup plain flour

Salt

20g butter

4 × 120g John Dory fillets

1 spring onion, green part only, finely sliced, for garnish

4 grilled lime halves (see recipe page 271), to serve

1. Roast capsicums in the oven or over a flame until partly charred. Place in a plastic bag and allow to sweat. Remove skin. Deseed and slice roasted capsicums into thin strips.

2. Slice half the onion and fry in a little oil until lightly browned. Finely chop remaining half and set aside. Add garlic and chilli to sliced onion in pan.

3. Add cream, Mexican oregano and capsicum and reduce heat. Simmer until cream is reduced to the point where it coats the back of a spoon.

4. Prepare refried beans by gently cooking the finely chopped onion in a little oil in a non-stick skillet until onion is transparent, without colouring. Add the diced pancetta. Add beans and epazote (if using), and cook for a minute or so. Using a wooden spoon, lightly squash beans to ensure they form a rough paste. Continue to cook until heated through.

5. Season flour with a little salt. Very lightly flour fish fillets.

6. Heat a little oil and butter until butter just begins to brown. Quickly fry fish fillets on both sides.

7. To serve, place fish on top of a portion of refried beans, and dress with sauce. Top with spring onion and serve with a grilled lime half on the side.

Crispy-skinned snapper with mushrooms, ginger and tropical fruit salsa

SERVES 4 | Recipe by Petra New

The perfect match of ginger and hoisin makes this simple stir-fry fish dish explosive in flavour. To achieve a crispy skin, do not turn the fish over until it is well and truly crisp.

TROPICAL FRUIT SALSA

¼ rock melon, diced
¼ honeydew melon, diced
½ small red onion, finely diced
1 tbsp chopped fresh mint
1 tbsp chopped fresh coriander
1 tbsp fish sauce
1 tbsp lime juice

4 × 180g snapper fillets, skin on
Cornflour, for dusting
60ml oil
3 cloves garlic, crushed
8cm fresh ginger, peeled and thinly sliced
6 shiitake mushrooms, sliced
1 tbsp hoisin sauce
80ml fish stock (see recipe page 272)
10ml fish sauce
1 tsp sugar
1 red chilli, deseeded and thinly sliced
½ tsp freshly ground pepper
1 spring onion, sliced, for garnish
Handful of coriander leaves, for garnish
4 cups freshly steamed rice, to serve

1. To make tropical fruit salsa, combine all ingredients in a serving bowl.

2. Dust fish fillets in a little cornflour and pan-fry for a few minutes each side in a little oil, skin-side down first. Remove, cover and keep warm.

3. Heat remaining oil in a wok or sauté pan over a medium heat and cook garlic, ginger and mushrooms for a couple of minutes.

4. Add hoisin sauce and fish stock and bring mix to the boil. Season with fish sauce and sugar. Finally, add chilli and black pepper.

5. Add fish fillets to sauce, flesh side down so that you don't ruin the crispy skin.

6. To serve, transfer the fish to a platter, and garnish with spring onion and coriander. Serve with salsa and rice on the side.

Snapper with green pea purée and crispy shrimp polenta

SERVES 4 | Recipe by Steve Roberts

This dish is a visual treat, not to mention an explosion of flavour.

SHRIMP POLENTA

150g instant polenta
20g Parmesan, grated
100g chopped cooked shrimp
1 tsp salt

PEA PURÉE

250g frozen peas
Salt and freshly ground pepper

Oil for frying
4 × 180g snapper fillets (or tarakihi or any
    other thin white fish fillet), skin on
Salt and freshly ground pepper
Oil, to sauté
1 medium fennel bulb, thinly sliced
Handful of watercress
1 tbsp capers
Juice of ½ lemon
4 cherry tomatoes, quartered

1. To make shrimp polenta, bring approximately 850ml of water to the boil in a saucepan and add polenta, mixing as you add. Cook for 5–10 minutes, stirring constantly. Add remaining ingredients and mix well.

2. Pour polenta onto an oiled tray. Leave to cool, then cut into 4 rounds.

3. Meanwhile, bring another pot of water to the boil to make pea purée. Add frozen peas and bring back to a simmer then drain, retaining some of the water.

4. Purée peas in a blender, adding a little of the blanching water to loosen the mix, and season.

5. Preheat oven to 180°C.

6. Lightly season snapper, then sear in a little oil in a hot pan skin-side down. Finish in the oven for approximately 3–5 minutes.

7. In a sauté pan with a little oil, reheat polenta rounds until golden.

8. Add fennel and watercress to a bowl. Rinse capers well and stir through. Squeeze over lemon juice and season to taste, then toss well.

9. On each serving plate, place some pea purée in the centre, top with a polenta round then a snapper fillet and garnish with fennel and cress salad and tomato quarters.

Balinese fried fish

SERVES 4 | Recipe by Petra New

Because it's deep-fried, this dish is very much in the 'sometimes', not the 'everyday' food group! Traditionally the whole fish would be used, including the head and tail.

2 large fish fillets

¼ tsp salt

Approximately ¼ cup rice flour, for coating

Oil for frying

1 large onion, sliced

½ tsp sambal oelek

1cm piece galangal, julienned

5cm piece lemongrass, white end, bruised and finely sliced

4 tbsp tamarind juice

¼ cup kecap manis

½ spring onion, sliced, including both green and white ends, for garnish

1. Cut each fish fillet into 4 even pieces. Season with salt and coat in rice flour, dusting off any excess.

2. Heat a deep-fryer to 190°C and cook fish pieces for 3–5 minutes, depending on thickness. Remove and drain on paper towel.

3. Heat a little oil in a pan and sauté onion until caramelised. Add sambal oelek, galangal and lemongrass and continue to cook until lemongrass has softened and is fragrant. Add tamarind juice and kecap manis and cook for a further 5 minutes.

4. Place fish on a serving platter and top with sauce. Garnish with spring onion.

Beer-battered fish fillets ▶

SERVES 4 | Recipe by Colin Doyle

Classic beer batter works perfectly with deep-fried fish. Serve with potato chips or wedges and a dollop of tomato sauce or tartare (see recipe page 266).

200g self-raising flour

1 egg, lightly beaten

375ml cold lager beer

Vegetable oil (e.g. canola or sunflower), for deep frying

4 × 160g white fish fillets (e.g. hoki, snapper, tarakihi or gurnard), skinned and boned

Salt and white pepper

¼ cup plain flour

4 grilled lemon halves (see recipe page 271), to serve

1. Mix self-raising flour and egg together in a bowl and slowly whisk in beer to create a batter consistency. Cover and leave to rest in the fridge for 15 minutes.

2. Heat oil in a deep-fryer or deep pan. Dry fish fillets with a paper towel. Season to taste. Lightly dust fish fillets with plain flour.

3. Dip floured fish fillets into batter, ensuring even coating. Leave excess to run off slightly and then carefully place in the hot oil.

4. Depending on the size of your deep-fryer or pan, add battered fillets, without crowding the pan. Cook for approximately 4 minutes (depending on fillet size) until batter is a crispy brown. Remove to an oven tray and keep warm in the oven while cooking the rest of the fish.

5. Serve with grilled lemon halves, chips and your choice of sauce.

Mixed seafood and vegetable stir-fry with cashew nuts

SERVES 4 | Recipe by Petra New

The best thing about a mixed seafood recipe is that you can easily change it to use whichever species are available, making it extremely cost-effective.

2 tbsp peanut oil

6 cloves garlic, crushed

1 onion, cut into large dice

1 long red chilli, deseeded and diced

1 carrot, cut into batons

2 courgettes, cut into batons

½ red capsicum, cut into batons

8 button mushrooms, quartered

500g fresh firm fish (e.g. kahawai, hapuku, kingfish), cut into large dice

1 tbsp fish sauce

1 tbsp soy sauce

2 tbsp crushed palm sugar

2 tbsp oyster sauce

¼ cup chicken stock

¾ cup basil leaves, picked

¼ cup chopped coriander

Juice of 1 lime

¼ cup cashew nuts, roasted

4 cups steamed jasmine rice, to serve

1. Heat a wok and add oil. Stir-fry garlic, onion and chilli until just starting to colour and become fragrant.

2. Add carrot, courgette, capsicum and mushrooms. Continue to stir-fry for 1 minute and then add fish cubes. Cook until medium–rare.

3. Add fish sauce, soy sauce, palm sugar, oyster sauce and chicken stock and bring to the boil. Add basil leaves and coriander, allowing to wilt slightly. Remove from heat and squeeze in lime juice.

4. Garnish with cashew nuts and serve with rice.

Bacon-wrapped salmon on portobello mushrooms

SERVES 4 | Recipe by Mark Dronjak

A great brunch dish to enjoy at the bach.

SUN-DRIED TOMATO AIOLI

2 tsp tomato paste

2 egg yolks

2 tbsp white wine vinegar

1 tsp creamy mustard (e.g. light Dijon)

Salt and freshly ground pepper

150–200ml light vegetable oil

50g sun-dried tomatoes, finely chopped

4 medium flat portobello mushrooms

Good-quality olive oil

4 × 100g salmon fillets

Sea salt and freshly ground black and
    white pepper

4 rashers streaky bacon

½ lemon, cut into thin wedges, to serve

1. Preheat oven to 180–200°C.

2. To make sun-dried tomato aioli, combine all ingredients except oil and sun-dried tomatoes in a large, very clean mixing bowl. Whisk together, then whisk oil into the bowl very slowly. Don't rush or the aioli will split (see Cook's Note below).

3. When aioli is ready, add sun-dried tomatoes and adjust seasoning to taste.

4. Place mushrooms in an oven dish with a splash of olive oil. Season to taste. Bake for 10–15 minutes. Alternatively, mushrooms could be cooked on a barbecue.

5. Season salmon fillets. Wrap each fillet in a rasher of bacon and sear on each side on the hot plate of a medium–hot barbecue with a little olive oil.

6. When salmon is cooked, serve each fillet on top of a mushroom and drizzle with aioli. Serve with lemon wedges.

COOK'S NOTE

If the aioli splits, add a little water to another large bowl and slowly drizzle in the split mix while whisking thoroughly.

Pan-fried hapuku with sautéed potatoes

SERVES 4 | Recipe by John Campbell

Crispy potatoes and spinach are topped with a grilled hapuku fillet and then a delicious citrus butter. Snapper would work equally as well as hapuku.

50ml olive oil

500g Agria potatoes, cooked in their skins and peeled when cool, then sliced

Salt and freshly ground pepper

40g butter

200g baby spinach

600g hapuku (or snapper)

50ml oil

80g butter

Juice of 2 limes or lemons

1 tbsp chopped fresh parsley

Splash of white wine

1. Heat a sauté pan with olive oil and, when hot, add sliced potatoes and brown, tossing from time to time. Season and add half the first measure of butter. Toss and set aside to keep warm.

2. To wilt spinach, melt second half of butter in a pot or sauté pan, add leaves and move them around for a few minutes, until cooked. Season to taste. If too wet, pat spinach dry on a tea towel or paper napkin.

3. Cut hapuku or snapper into even-sized portions.

4. Heat a large sauté pan with the oil. Add fish to the pan, then seal and brown for approximately 3 minutes, skin-side up. Turn fish over, add one-third of the second measure of butter and cook through (approximately another 3 minutes).

5. Remove fish and set aside to keep warm.

6. Add remaining butter to the pan. When foaming, add lime or lemon juice, parsley and wine to create a sauce.

7. Place sautéed potatoes and spinach on a serving plate and top with fish and citrus sauce.

Seared tuna rolls with seaweed salad

SERVES 4 | Recipe by Steve Roberts

Seared tuna with the crunch of the seaweed salad makes this dish an excellent contrast in textures, not to mention flavours.

200g sushi-grade tuna loin

1 tsp shichimi togarashi (Japanese spice mix available from Asian supermarkets)

Salt

Oil for frying

4 rice paper wrappers

60g marinated seaweed salad (available from Asian supermarkets and specialty stores)

1 tsp wasabi powder

70ml Japanese mayonnaise

Handful of mixed Asian micro greens, for garnish

1. Season tuna with togarashi and salt, then quickly sear in a hot pan in a little oil on all sides. Remove and cool in the refrigerator.

2. Fill a wide bowl with warm water. Place in sheets of rice paper, one at a time, and allow to soften, then remove and place on a clean tea towel to soak up excess water.

3. Slice chilled tuna loin and place some in the centre of a sheet of rice paper, arrange some seaweed salad on top and roll up tightly. Repeat with remaining rice paper wrappers. Cover with a damp cloth and refrigerate until serving.

4. Mix together wasabi and mayonnaise.

5. To serve, slice the rolls into 2cm thick slices, then zigzag mayonnaise onto the slices. Top each with micro greens.

Sweet and sour wok-fried crab

SERVES 4 | Recipe by Petra New

Be prepared to get a bit messy – the results will be worth it!

2 large whole crabs

Canola oil

1 large onion, chopped into large dice

1 cup cubed pineapple

SWEET AND SOUR SAUCE

Juice of 1 lime

3 tbsp white sugar

1 tbsp fish sauce

1 tbsp oyster sauce

1 tbsp soy sauce

1 tbsp tomato sauce

1. Wash each crab under cold running water.

2. Lay each crab out in front of you. Place one hand over one side of the claws and pull the shell of the crab off. Remove spongy gills and stomach. Turn crab over and remove the smaller shell at the base of the crab and the mouth and small claws. Remove both front claws and break each into two pieces. Cut crab in half through the middle. Cut each half into three pieces, making sure you have a claw or two with each piece.

3. Heat a wok over a medium–high heat, add a little canola oil and stir-fry crab, then remove and set aside.

4. Add onion and sauté until translucent. Add pineapple and cooked crab to the wok.

5. Mix together sweet and sour sauce ingredients and pour over crab. Continue to stir-fry for another minute or until sauce is bubbly and glossy.

6. Serve on a large platter.

DID YOU KNOW?

The geoduck is a very large saltwater clam, with the shell growing between 15–25cm in length, and an extremely long 'neck' or siphon. Due to an increase in demand the geoduck are now farmed as well as harvested in the wild. The 'neck' meat has a slightly crunchy texture and can be poached in a savoury broth, sautéed in butter and blended with Asian flavours or eaten raw sashimi-style with chilli dipping sauce.

Crispy-skinned snapper with red capsicum and fennel confit and black olive tapenade

SERVES 4 | Recipe by Marco Edwardes

Also ideal for barbecue cooking. Great with all kinds of seafood.

RED CAPSICUM AND FENNEL CONFIT

2 red capsicums

½ head garlic (peel and leave cloves whole)

4 sprigs fresh thyme

3 sprigs fresh rosemary

2 fennel bulbs, finely shredded

75ml olive oil

10 fresh basil leaves, shredded

Sea salt and freshly ground pepper

BLACK OLIVE TAPENADE

150g pitted black olives

4 anchovy fillets in olive oil (optional)

2 tsp capers, drained and rinsed

1 clove garlic

2 tbsp olive oil

4 × 150g snapper fillets, skin on (or 2 whole snapper, gutted and scaled)

50ml olive oil

50g butter

Juice of ½ lemon

1 lemon, cut into wedges, to serve

Fresh chervil or dill, for garnish

1. Preheat oven to 200°C.

2. To prepare red capsicum and fennel confit, put capsicums on a baking tray, scatter with garlic, thyme and rosemary and then bake in the preheated oven for approximately 10 minutes until the capsicum skin starts to blister. Discard garlic, thyme and rosemary.

3. Remove capsicums from oven, place in a bowl and cover tightly with cling film. Leave to rest for about 10 minutes.

4. Remove skin from capsicums and cut flesh into strips.

5. Sauté shredded fennel in olive oil until soft. Add capsicum strips and shredded basil leaves to the pan. Season to taste and set aside.

6. To make black olive tapenade, blend all the ingredients in a food processor until smooth. Place in a small bowl.

7. Season snapper skin with salt and pepper. Heat olive oil in a large non-stick frying pan, add snapper skin-side down and cook for 1½–2 minutes until golden and crisp. Turn and cook flesh side for 30–60 seconds until just firm. Remove fish from the pan and keep warm.

8. Add butter to the pan and heat until golden. Add lemon juice and allow to heat, then pour over fish fillets.

9. To serve, divide confit between 4 plates and place fish on top. Place a quenelle of olive tapenade on the side. Garnish with lemon wedges and chervil or dill.

COOK'S NOTE

If making more tapenade than required, place in a clean jar and cover with a thin layer of olive oil, seal with a lid and place in the fridge for up to a week.

Market fish with butterbean purée, scallops and chorizo with salsa verde

SERVES 4 | Recipe by Steve Roberts

Crispy pan-roasted fish, creamy butterbean purée and scallops are balanced by the bite from the chorizo. Finished with salsa verde, this is a simple dish but packed with flavour.

SALSA VERDE

60g capers
Good handful of fresh basil leaves
Good handful of flat-leaf parsley
Small handful of fresh mint
2 cloves garlic
1 tsp Dijon mustard
Juice of 1 lemon
Olive oil
Salt and freshly ground pepper

BUTTERBEAN PURÉE

450g cooked butterbeans (or canned, rinsed well)
50ml fish stock (see recipe page 272)
1 clove garlic, crushed
50ml olive oil
Salt and freshly ground pepper

2 chorizo sausages, thinly sliced
12 cherry tomatoes, chopped
Extra virgin olive oil
Salt and freshly ground pepper
4 × 160–180g market-fresh fish fillets (e.g. bluenose, hapuku or snapper), skin on, cut in half
12 scallops
1 spring onion, green end only, julienned, for garnish
1 tbsp balsamic reduction (see glossary page 276)

1. To make salsa verde, wash capers well to remove saltiness. Combine them with all ingredients except olive oil and seasoning in a food processor. Process mixture, adding olive oil to produce a smooth purée. Season to taste.

2. To make butterbean purée, purée all ingredients except seasoning in a food processor then pass through a sieve. Season to taste.

3. Fry chorizo and tomato in a little olive oil until chorizo is crisp, then remove from pan.

4. Season fish and fry in the chorizo oil for a few minutes each side, starting skin-side down, until crispy; remove and set aside. Quickly sauté scallops in the same oil.

5. In a saucepan gently reheat butterbean purée and place a spoonful in the centre of each serving plate. Layer fish and chorizo with tomato, with 2 pieces of fish per plate; garnish with spring onion. Place scallops beside fish and top with salsa verde, then drizzle around balsamic reduction.

Snapper on curry-spiced cauliflower florets with coconut cream and lychee foam

SERVES 4 | Recipe by Mark Dronjak

Exotic, fresh and sophisticated. A touch of the tropics meets Asia.

½ white cauliflower, cut into florets

250g canned lychees (juice retained)

250ml coconut cream

50ml cream

Sea salt and freshly ground pepper

1 large egg, white only

Olive oil

50g butter

4 × 150g snapper fillets (or tarakihi or ling), skin on

1–2 tsp turmeric

1–2 tsp Madras curry powder (mild)

100g micro greens (or edible flowers such as Thai basil, chive or borage flowers)

1. In a large pot blanch cauliflower florets, taking care not to overcook, until just al dente. Refresh in cold water, dry and set aside.

2. Cut half the lychees in two and keep the remaining ones whole. Place lychee halves and half of the whole lychees in a small pan with coconut cream and half of the cream. Place over a low heat and simmer to keep warm. Season to taste. Add remaining cream just prior to serving to add a shine.

3. Blend egg white in a food processor or blender until half whipped. Add a little lychee juice to taste. Whisk fully to form the lychee foam.

4. Heat a flat pan for fish, add a splash of olive oil and half the butter. Season snapper fillets and cook for a few minutes each side, presentation-side down first. If not cooked through, finish in a hot oven.

5. In a sauté pan or small saucepan, heat remaining butter and a little olive oil. Add cauliflower florets, turmeric (a little at a time and to taste) and curry powder (a little at a time and to taste). Sauté for a few minutes, adding colour but taking care not to burn the spices. Season to taste.

6. To serve, place cauliflower on the plates, drizzle with a little sauce and place snapper on top. Spoon lychee foam around the plates. Place remaining few whole lychees around the plates as garnish. Use a few micro greens (or flowers) for garnish.

Eggs Benedict with salmon on kumara cakes and orange Hollandaise

SERVES 4 | Recipe by Petra New

Kumara and orange go fantastically well together and the citrus helps cut through the creaminess of the Hollandaise and the salmon.

ORANGE HOLLANDAISE

300ml fresh orange juice

3 egg yolks

200g melted butter

1 tsp white vinegar

Salt and freshly ground pepper

KUMARA CAKES

2 medium kumara

¼ leek, chopped

Olive oil

1 small egg, beaten

Salt and freshly ground pepper

Cooking spray

4 × 150g salmon fillets

Salt and freshly ground pepper

4 large eggs

1 tbsp white vinegar

1. To make orange Hollandaise reduce orange juice by two-thirds by simmering in a small pot.

2. In a heatproof bowl, beat egg yolks with a whisk. Place bowl over a pot of hot water (making sure the bowl does not touch the water) and whisk until slightly thick ('ribbon stage').

3. Remove from heat and cool. Slowly add butter while continually whisking. Whisk in orange juice and vinegar and season. If the sauce splits, whisk an egg yolk in a separate bowl and slowly add the split sauce to the yolk.

4. To make kumara cakes, peel and dice kumara and place in a pot of salted water over medium heat and cook until soft. Drain well.

5. Sauté leek in a splash of olive oil until cooked and lightly coloured. Add kumara and allow the mix to completely dry out – it needs to be very dry. Roughly mash, then add egg. Season and mix well. Mould into 4 cakes and set aside.

6. Place a barbecue liner on the barbecue plate. Heat to medium. Spray liner with cooking spray and arrange salmon fillet on it flesh-side down. Season. Place kumara cakes on the liner and cook until brown on each side. Turn salmon and season the other side.

7. Meanwhile, poach eggs in simmering water with vinegar added. Set them aside on a tea towel.

8. To serve, place a kumara cake on each plate, top with salmon and then a poached egg. Spoon over the Hollandaise sauce.

Pan-fried broadbill in a saffron sauce

SERVES 4 | Recipe by John Campbell

This creamy saffron sauce goes well with any chunky oily fish.

SAUCE

½ tsp saffron threads

300ml white wine

50ml olive oil

2 cloves garlic, chopped

100g onion, chopped

Sliced bread with no crusts, cubed

¼ tsp cumin

Salt and freshly ground pepper

Olive oil for frying

100g raw prawn cutlets

600g broadbill fillets

2 tbsp chopped fresh parsley, for garnish

1 lemon, cut into wedges, to serve

Good-quality olive oil, for drizzling

1. To make sauce, soak saffron in wine while you heat a pan with oil.

2. Gently fry garlic and onion in the pan for 3–4 minutes until soft.

3. Add bread and brown slightly. Remove from heat, then add wine with saffron and cumin. Season and blend in a processor or with a hand-held blender.

4. In a large pan heat some olive oil and cook prawns for a couple of minutes, until pink, then remove and set aside. Place broadbill in the pan, turning once after 3 minutes cooking. Add sauce to the pan, season and cook for a few more minutes. Add sealed prawns. If sauce reduces too much, add a little water.

5. To serve, place fish on a plate and top with prawns and sauce. Garnish with parsley and lemon wedges and a drizzle of olive oil.

Pies, casseroles, bakes and steamed and one-pot meals

Fish tartlets with fresh herbs   204

Moroccan-baked chermoula fish with couscous   206

Mediterranean-inspired whole baked fish   208

Eggplant-topped fish fillets with carrot fritters and dill yoghurt   209

Gratin of white fish, scallops and prawns with karengo   210

Kingfish with a Mexican spice paste baked in banana leaves   212

Fish and tomato Spanish-style stew   214

Jambalaya   214

Hot-smoked broadbill with mash and caper sauce   215

Seafood and chorizo with fava beans   216

Thai red curry with fish   216

Salmon and spinach filo pie   218

Seafood gumbo   219

Salmon with caper and olive dressing   220

Smoked fish and spinach pies   220

Whole snapper steamed with ginger, basil and chilli   222

Trevally baked in a citrus salt crust with mustard and tarragon aioli   224

Scallop and potato Panang curry   225

Smoked fish pies   226

Market fish with eggplant, tomato and mozzarella   228

Poached monkfish in potato and tomato casserole   228

Baked market fish with white bean purée, fennel salad and orange oil   231

Bengali-style fish curry   232

Baked fish with Mediterranean crumble   234

Mussels steamed in Thai red curry with citrus   234

Baked white fish with Pernod cream sauce and potatoes   236

Fish pie with puff pastry   237

Tea-steamed salmon with Thai red curry and coconut cream emulsion   238

Fish tartlets with fresh herbs

MAKES 4 × 12CM TARTLETS | Recipe by Colin Doyle

This recipe calls for monkfish, which has a firm texture and a flavour similar to crayfish. You could use another fish with a little sweetness such as gurnard or a little crabmeat, if wished. You can also use this recipe to make a single 23cm tart.

PASTRY

125g butter

125g cream cheese

1 cup plain flour, sifted

2 shallots, finely diced

140g Gruyère cheese, grated

200g monkfish, thinly sliced

3 eggs

½ cup cream

1 tsp chopped fresh tarragon

1 tbsp chopped fresh chives

1 tbsp chopped fresh parsley

Salt and white pepper

1. Prepare pastry by creaming butter and cream cheese together. Add sifted flour and mix until dough comes together. Wrap in cling film and chill for at least 20 minutes.

2. Preheat oven to 200°C.

3. Roll out pastry to approximately 6mm thick and cut discs to fit four 12cm fluted tartlet cases. Prick the bases lightly with a fork and place empty cases into the oven for 10 minutes. Remove from oven and place on an oven tray.

4. When cases have cooled slightly, divide shallots, Gruyère and monkfish between the cases.

5. Lightly beat eggs with cream and chopped herbs in a jug. Season to taste. Pour mixture into the cases, filling to within 5mm of the top.

6. Bake for 7 minutes, then reduce heat to 150°C and cook for another 25–30 minutes or until set.

COOK'S NOTE

This amount of dough will also make a 23cm pie dish, so a single large tart would be an alternative to the individual servings. If making a large tart, you can omit the blind baking of the case and cook the tart at 200°C for the first 10 minutes and then 150°C for about 35–40 minutes.

Moroccan-baked chermoula fish with couscous

SERVES 4 | Recipe by John Campbell

The herbs and spices in this chermoula create a wonderful Moroccan flavour that goes well with any white fish fillet.

CHERMOULA DRESSING

2 cloves garlic, chopped

1 fresh red chilli, chopped, or ½ tsp chopped dry chillies

½ tsp paprika

¼ cup chopped parsley

¼ cup chopped coriander

1 tsp ground cumin

Juice of 1 lemon

80–100ml olive oil

Salt and freshly ground pepper

COUSCOUS

300g instant couscous

300g warm water or stock

Zest of ½ preserved lemon (see recipe page 271)

¼ cup chopped sun-dried tomato

¼ cup chopped parsley

1½ tbsp olive oil

Sea salt and freshly ground pepper

Cooking spray

700g market-fresh fish fillets

Few cumin seeds, for garnish

4 grilled lemon halves (see recipe page 271), to serve

1. To make chermoula dressing, place all ingredients into a food processor or bowl with a stick blender and blend to create a paste.

2. Place couscous in a dish and cover with warm water or stock.

3. Cover with cling film and leave for 15–20 minutes.

4. Remove cling film and mix in other ingredients.

5. Preheat oven to 220°C. Spray an oven tray or baking dish with oil.

6. Place a little dressing on the tray, then place fish on top. Spoon dressing over fish so that it's well covered, retaining some for serving.

7. Bake for approximately 6 minutes, basting a couple of times during cooking.

8. Serve on couscous with a dab of the remaining dressing over the fish. Sprinkle with some cumin seeds. Accompany with grilled lemon halves.

DID YOU KNOW?

The red cod has a barbel – a protruding fleshy filament – on its lower jaw, which it uses to detect prey buried in mud or sand.

Mediterranean-inspired whole baked fish

SERVES 4 | Recipe by Petra New

A whole baked fish brought to the table creates a great 'wow' factor. This classic combination of olives, tomatoes, basil and garlic seep through the fish to create a moist and full-of-flavour dish.

1.5kg whole fish (e.g. tarakihi or snapper, weight after the gut has been removed), scaled

4 tomatoes

Olive oil

3 cloves garlic, sliced

1 red onion, diced

¼ preserved lemon (see recipe page 271), skin only, diced

½ cup Kalamata olives, pitted

¼ cup fresh basil leaves

Salt and freshly ground pepper

100g feta

1 tbsp chopped parsley

1. Lightly rinse fish. Wipe the inside and outside with a tea towel to remove any scales and blood that may still be on the fish.

2. Bring a pot of water to the boil. Make a cross in the bottom of each tomato with a knife and place in the boiling water for 20 seconds, then plunge into iced water. Remove skin and seeds, then dice flesh.

3. Heat a pan and add some olive oil. Sauté garlic and onion until transparent and fragrant. Remove from heat.

4. In a bowl, combine tomato, garlic, onion, preserved lemon skin, olives and basil. Toss with a little olive oil and season.

5. Preheat oven to 180°C.

6. Place fish on a sheet of pre-greased tin foil. Stuff cavity with the tomato mixture, reserving ¼ cup. Wrap fish in the tin foil and bake for approximately 30 minutes.

7. Carefully open the top of the tin foil and check fish is cooked.

8. Top fish with the remaining tomato mixture and crumble over feta. Place under a hot grill until feta browns slightly.

9. Serve on a platter. Sprinkle with chopped parsley and a drizzle of olive oil.

DID YOU KNOW?

Tarakihi is one of the top fish for Kiwi consumers. For many years, it was New Zealand's second most important commercial catch.

Eggplant-topped fish fillets with carrot fritters and dill yoghurt

SERVES 4 | Recipe by Petra New

Courgettes would work just as well for the fritters.

½ eggplant
Salt
Extra virgin olive oil
4 cloves garlic, crushed
½ cup fresh breadcrumbs
Salt and freshly ground pepper
4 × 180g fish fillets, boned

CARROT FRITTERS

2 carrots, grated and squeezed to remove excess moisture
1 tsp fennel seeds, dry-roasted and crushed
1 spring onion, finely sliced
½ cup self-raising flour
1 large egg, beaten
Salt and freshly ground pepper
100ml milk (more or less)
Oil for cooking

DILL YOGHURT

1 cup thick plain unsweetened yoghurt
2 tbsp chopped dill
Zest of 1 lemon
Salt and freshly ground pepper

1. Slice eggplant, sprinkle with salt and set aside for 30 minutes to allow any bitterness to seep out. Gently wipe the slices with a tea towel. Place in a bowl and drizzle with extra virgin olive oil and half of the crushed garlic.

2. Barbecue eggplant on the chargrill until tender. Remove and allow to cool, then finely dice.

3. Preheat oven to fanbake 220°C.

4. In a bowl, combine eggplant, breadcrumbs and remaining crushed garlic. Season and drizzle with extra virgin olive oil to form a light, moist crumb.

5. Place fish fillets in a baking dish lined with baking paper and sprinkle evenly with crumb mixture. Bake for 8–12 minutes (depending on thickness of fish).

6. To make carrot fritters while fish is baking, place grated carrot in a bowl. Add fennel seeds and spring onion. Toss to combine, and then add flour and egg. Season to taste and add enough milk to form a light batter. Mix well.

7. Place a barbecue liner on the hot plate, drizzle with oil and place spoonfuls of the carrot batter onto the liner. Cook fritters until small bubbles appear and start to pop, then turn over and cook all the way through.

8. To make dill yoghurt, mix together yoghurt, dill and lemon zest. Season to taste.

9. To serve, place 2–3 carrot fritters on each plate. Top with a fish fillet and a dollop of dill yoghurt.

DID YOU KNOW?
Orange roughy species were originally called 'slimeheads'. They got a name change to 'orange roughy' in the 1970s.

Gratin of white fish, scallops and prawns with karengo

SERVES 4 | Recipe by John Campbell

Seafood blended with local herbs, cream and butter and grilled to perfection.

400ml fish stock (see recipe page 272)

1 tbsp karengo (see glossary page 276)

2 shallots, finely diced

200ml cream

50ml extra virgin olive oil

300g firm white fish (e.g. hapuku, gurnard, boar fish), cut into large dice

100g scallops

100g prawns

1 head broccoli, cut into small pieces and blanched

200g purple Maori potatoes, cooked and diced

30g butter

100g Parmesan, grated

Sprinkle of kawakawa (see glossary page 276)

Salt and New York cut black pepper (see glossary page 276) or freshly ground pepper

1. Preheat oven to 230°C grill.

2. In a good-sized pan heat fish stock, karengo and shallots to reduce by half. Add cream and reduce by about half again. Set aside.

3. Heat oil in a large ovenproof pan on the stovetop and sauté seafood for a few minutes, in batches if necessary.

4. Add broccoli and potato to the pan. Season to taste.

5. Reheat sauce. Add butter and combine.

6. Pour sauce over seafood and vegetables in the pan. Sprinkle with Parmesan, kawakawa and pepper and grill for 3–4 minutes.

7. Serve from the pan.

DID YOU KNOW?

Fishers have often known red gurnard to grunt when caught. Recent sound studies in the Leigh Marine Reserve have shown that the fish makes a surprisingly wide range of vocalisations in its daily life.

Kingfish with a Mexican spice paste baked in banana leaves

SERVES 5 | Recipe by Colin Doyle

The ground annatto seeds in this spice paste, or achiote, give an earthy, intriguing flavour and brick-red colour, while baking the fish in a banana leaf keeps the fish moist. The paste will improve in flavour if made a day ahead.

MEXICAN SPICE PASTE

45g annatto seeds

2 whole allspice berries

1 tsp black peppercorns

2 whole cloves

1 tbsp ground coriander

1 tsp ground cumin

Pinch of ground cinnamon

1 tbsp dried Mexican oregano (available from specialty stores)

6 cloves garlic

1 tsp salt

1½ tsp cornflour

Juice of 3 oranges

3 tbsp white vinegar

1 cup long-grain rice

½ tbsp chicken stock powder

1 small white onion, finely diced

Olive oil

Small handful of fresh coriander, finely chopped

5 banana leaves (each at least 25cm square)

5 × 120g portions kingfish steaks or fillets

Olive oil

2–3 corn tortillas per person (see recipe page 272), to serve

1. To make Mexican spice paste, grind whole spices using a mortar and pestle until fine. It is easier to do this in several batches, rather than all at once. Add coriander, cumin, cinnamon and oregano and mix well. Set aside in a bowl.

2. Grind together garlic and salt to form a fine paste. Add ground spices and cornflour, followed by orange juice and vinegar, a little at a time to make a smooth paste.

3. Rinse rice and put in a pot with a tight-fitting lid. Add stock powder, onion, a dash of oil, coriander and 2 cups of water. Bring rice to the boil, uncovered, then simmer for 5 minutes. Cover and turn off heat. The rice will absorb any remaining liquid and will be ready in 20 minutes.

4. Soften banana leaves by waving over the flame of the gas hob or putting them in the microwave. Place leaves on top of a larger sheet of foil. Coat fish portions in spice paste. Wrap each portion in a banana leaf with a splash of oil, then wrap in foil. Leave for up to 1 hour to marinate before cooking.

5. Preheat oven to 180°C.

6. Place wrapped portions on a tray and bake for 20 minutes.

7. Serve on the banana leaf with rice and corn tortillas on the side.

Fish and tomato Spanish-style stew

SERVES 4 | Recipe by Petra New

Most stews take a lot of cooking time, but this is one of the quickest you will ever make.

Extra virgin olive oil
½ onion, diced
½ yellow capsicum, diced
2 cloves garlic, crushed
100ml white wine
200g canned crushed tomatoes
1 bay leaf
1 tsp brown sugar
2 sprigs fresh thyme
200g hapuku, skinned and boned, diced
Salt and freshly ground pepper
2 tbsp chopped flat-leaf parsley

1. Heat oil in a pan and sauté onion, capsicum and garlic until fragrant.

2. Deglaze pan with wine. Reduce by half and add tomatoes along with bay leaf, sugar and thyme. Cook for 5 minutes.

3. Add hapuku. Cook for a further 5 minutes. Season to taste.

4. Remove from heat. Gently mix through parsley so that you do not flake up the fish. Remove bay leaf and thyme stalks.

5. Serve with crusty bread.

Jambalaya

SERVES 4 | Recipe by John Campbell

Serve this on a large platter to maximise the colours and textures.

1 tbsp canola oil
1 onion, diced
3 cloves garlic, crushed
100g chicken breast, diced
1 tsp each smoked paprika, cayenne pepper, freshly
    ground pepper
½ tsp white pepper
1 tsp chopped fresh thyme
¼ cup chopped parsley, plus extra for garnish
100g thick ham (e.g. ham steak), diced
1 chorizo sausage, sliced
1 stalk celery, finely diced
½ green capsicum, diced
2 cups long-grain rice
3 cups chicken stock
400g can whole peeled tomatoes
Salt and freshly ground pepper
16 raw prawns, in the shell

1. Heat oil in a large lidded pan. Sauté onion and garlic until soft. Add chicken, sealing all sides. Mix in spices and herbs. Cook for 2 minutes, until fragrant. Add ham, chorizo, celery and capsicum. Cook for 5 minutes.

2. Sprinkle over rice. Add chicken stock and tomatoes. Bring to the boil, cover and cook over medium heat for 10 minutes. Stir and season. Add prawns. Cover and cook for a further 10 minutes or until rice is cooked through.

3. Serve sprinkled with chopped parsley.

Hot-smoked broadbill with mash and caper sauce

SERVES 4 | Recipe by John Campbell

This great smoked fish recipe will suit any chunky oily fish. Marinated with citrus and Cajun spices, and topped with a creamy caper sauce, it is delicious! You can use your barbecue if it has a hood, but don't have too much heat around the fish.

MARINADE

50ml Kikkoman soy sauce
Zest and juice of 1 lime
2 cloves garlic, chopped
2 tsp chopped thyme
1 tsp Cajun spice mix (see recipe page 261)
1 tbsp brown sugar

4 × 170g broadbill fillets, skin on

CAPER SAUCE

300ml fish stock (see recipe page 272)
1½ tbsp cream
3 tbsp capers
2 tsp chopped fresh dill
Salt and freshly ground pepper

300g new potatoes, unpeeled
Salt and freshly ground pepper
Olive oil
⅓ cup wood chips, for cooking

1. Mix all marinade ingredients together in a bowl.

2. Spread marinade over fish fillets and leave for 20 minutes.

3. To make caper sauce, heat fish stock in a pan and reduce by half. Add cream and reduce again by half. Add capers and chopped dill. Season to taste.

4. Preheat oven to 250°C. Do not use fanbake.

5. Cook potatoes, then roughly mash with seasoning and a little olive oil. Keep warm.

6. Place marinated broadbill fillets on a greased tray.

7. Turn on the extractor fan in your kitchen. Place wood chips in an old pan and heat on the stovetop until smoking, then place in the bottom of the oven (not on a rack).

8. Place fish in the centre of the oven for 6–8 minutes, depending on the thickness of the fish.

9. Serve fish in shallow bowls on top on mash with sauce drizzled over.

Seafood and chorizo with fava beans

SERVES 4 | Recipe by Mark Dronjak

Spanish influences create great flavours.

Olive oil
3 cloves garlic, finely crushed
12 mussels, cleaned
12 fresh cockles or clams, purged
Pinch of saffron
200ml fish stock (see recipe page 272)
250ml dry apple cider
100ml dry white wine
Sea salt and freshly ground pepper
1 chorizo sausage, sliced
12 prawns
2 squid tubes, sliced
250g canned fava beans, drained and rinsed
1 tsp smoked paprika
4 tbsp finely chopped parsley, for garnish

1. Heat a wide-bottomed lidded pan and add a good splash of olive oil. Add garlic, mussels and cockles or clams. Cover and cook until shellfish have opened, then set them aside. Discard any that don't open.

2. To the same pan, add saffron, fish stock, cider and white wine and quickly simmer until liquid has reduced by a third. Adjust seasoning.

3. Add chorizo, heat slightly then add prawns, squid, fava beans and smoked paprika. Return the shellfish to the pan to reheat. Season to taste.

4. Garnish with parsley and serve.

Thai red curry with fish ▶

SERVES 4 | Recipe by Petra New

Look for fatter fillets, as you want the chunks of fish to be visible in this curry.

2 tbsp peanut oil
2 tbsp Thai red curry paste (see recipe page 271)
200ml coconut cream
¼ large purple eggplant, cubed
50g canned bamboo shoots
4 Kaffir lime leaves
200ml coconut milk
2 tbsp fish sauce
600g firm white fish (e.g. hapuku, kingfish, monkfish), cut into chunks
1 cup fresh basil leaves, chopped
Juice of 1 lime
Handful of coriander leaves, for garnish
4 cups freshly steamed rice, to serve

1. Heat oil and stir-fry curry paste for 2 minutes. Add coconut cream (reserving 2 tablespoons for garnish) and bring to the boil. Add eggplant, bamboo shoots and Kaffir lime leaves and cook for 2 minutes. Add coconut milk and simmer until eggplant is soft.

2. Add fish sauce and turn the heat back up. Add fish and cook for 4 minutes. Remove from the heat and add basil leaves so that they just wilt. Add lime juice.

3. To serve, garnish with coriander and a drizzle of reserved coconut cream. Serve with rice.

Salmon and spinach filo pie

SERVES 4 | Recipe by Colin Doyle

Golden layers of flaky filo yield a luscious salmon with a tasty spinach and mushroom filling. The herb and mustard cream sauce is a delicious complement.

500g salmon fillet, skin off

100g spinach

6 button mushrooms, finely diced

3 shallots, finely diced

50g butter

Salt and freshly ground pepper

1 package filo pastry

SAUCE

¼ cup white wine

2 tbsp white vinegar

2 tbsp Dijon mustard

250ml cream

1 tbsp chopped fresh tarragon

1 tbsp chopped fresh dill

1. Slice salmon in half to make 2 pieces of the same shape that can be stacked on top of each other.

2. Blanch spinach in boiling water, drain well and dry with a tea towel. Finely chop.

3. Cook mushrooms and shallots with 1 tablespoon butter until mixture is dry. Season to taste.

4. Preheat oven to 180°C.

5. Lay out a sheet of filo pastry on a work surface. You will need a piece approximately twice the length and width of the salmon pieces. You may need to overlap 2 sheets to make it large enough to fully enclose salmon.

6. Season both salmon fillets and place one in the centre of the pastry. Top with half the cooked mushrooms, then spinach and then remaining mushrooms. Top with the second piece of salmon. Wrap salmon in pastry, then melt remaining butter and brush on top. Wrap a second sheet of filo around the parcel, alternating the direction of the wrapping, so that the salmon is well contained. Repeat wrapping until there are 6 layers in total.

7. Place on a baking tray and bake for 40 minutes.

8. While salmon is baking, make the sauce by heating wine and vinegar in a pot, reducing it by half. Stir in mustard and cream and simmer until it is reduced and thickens slightly. Cool slightly before stirring in herbs.

9. To serve, slice up the salmon parcel and serve drizzled with sauce.

Seafood gumbo

SERVES 4 | Recipe by John Campbell

The roux and Cajun spice take this seafood blend up a notch. Make it as spicy as you can handle.

ROUX

1 cup vegetable oil

¾ cup plain flour

30ml oil

100g onion, diced

200g capsicum, diced

3 cloves garlic, finely diced

500ml chicken stock

1 bay leaf

½ tsp freshly ground pepper

¼ tsp cayenne pepper

½ tsp Cajun spice mix (see recipe page 261)

Splash of Tabasco sauce

400g can peeled tomatoes

300g shellfish (e.g. scallops, crab, oysters, prawns)

Salt

Chopped parsley, for garnish

4 cups cooked plain rice , to serve

1. To make roux, heat a heavy-based pot (not Teflon) on low. Add 4 parts oil and 3 parts flour to make 120g of roux. Cook on low for approximately 30–40 minutes until you have a brown, nutty roux. Keep an eye on it during browning as it can catch and burn easily.

2. Heat a 3–4 litre pot with half the oil and cook onion, capsicum and garlic until transparent, without colouring.

3. Add roux and then add stock slowly, as you would when making a white sauce. Add bay leaf, spices and Tabasco. (Only add as much pepper seasoning as you like or can handle.)

4. Chop tomatoes and add flesh and juice to the pot. Continue to cook mixture slowly.

5. In a separate pan, add the rest of the oil and when hot sauté seafood. Set aside until required.

6. Adjust gumbo seasoning – it should be pepper hot.

7. Add seafood and serve with a sprinkle of parsley and rice on the side.

Salmon with caper and olive dressing

SERVES 4 | Recipe by Mark Dronjak

A great, balanced salmon dish.

4 × 150g ocean-fresh salmon fillets
Sea salt and freshly ground pepper

CAPER AND OLIVE DRESSING
75g pitted green olives, finely chopped
75g capers
4 tbsp finely chopped flat-leaf parsley
Juice of 1–2 lemons (about 50ml)
50ml good-quality lemon-infused olive oil
2 tbsp good-quality extra virgin olive oil
1 spring onion, finely chopped
Sea salt and freshly ground pepper
1–2 tsp white sugar (if required)

Extra virgin olive oil
1 lemon, cut into wedges, to serve

1. Preheat oven to 200°C.
2. Season salmon to taste.
3. To make caper and olive dressing, combine all ingredients in a small saucepan on a very low heat and warm gently. Season to taste and add sugar if required.
4. Place salmon on an oven tray. Drizzle with olive oil and cook for 10–15 minutes. Do not overcook.
5. Remove salmon from the oven and serve with dressing. Garnish with lemon wedges.

Smoked fish and spinach pies ▶

SERVES 4 AS A STARTER | Recipe by John Campbell

Also known as 'smokies', these make a great starter dish.

350g spinach, trimmed
400g fresh smoked snapper, tarakihi or hapuku
¼ cup cream
50g butter
A little freshly grated nutmeg
White pepper
Hollandaise sauce (see recipe page 265)

1. Preheat oven to grill 250°C.
2. Blanch and refresh spinach leaves.
3. Break smoked fish into chunky pieces and warm in a pot with cream.
4. Heat a frying pan over a moderate heat and add butter, then spinach. Stir with a fork and add a sprinkling of nutmeg and seasoning.
5. Place some of the spinach in a ramekin or small entrée bowl. Fill three-quarters of the bowl with smoked fish. Top with a little Hollandaise sauce and place under hot grill for approximately 1 minute to glaze.
6. Serve at once.

Whole snapper steamed with ginger, basil and chilli

SERVES 4 | Recipe by Petra New

Steaming is a fantastic way to cook whole fish, as it locks in the moisture.

2 small–medium whole snapper, scaled and gutted

2cm piece ginger, grated

2 cloves garlic, crushed

½ long red chilli, deseeded (optional) and chopped

1 lemon, sliced

½ cup fresh basil leaves, chopped

SAUCE

1 tsp peanut oil

2 small shallots

1cm piece ginger, grated

½ long red chilli, deseeded (optional) and chopped

3 tbsp soy sauce

3 tbsp fish sauce

1 cup chicken stock

1 tbsp palm sugar

1 tsp cornflour

¼ cup fresh basil leaves

1 tbsp chopped fresh coriander leaves

1. Wipe inside and outside of each fish with a damp tea towel to remove any scales and blood that may still be on fish.

2. Make 3 deep score marks on both sides of each fish to allow it to cook more evenly and the flavours to penetrate the fish while cooking.

3. Rub ginger, garlic and chilli into the outside flesh.

4. Fill cavity with lemon slices and half the basil, and scatter remaining basil over fish.

5. Place fish into a steamer half filled with water on a medium–high heat steam for at least 10–15 minutes, depending on the size of the fish. Test it by pulling a little away from the bone – it should come away without resistance.

6. To make sauce, heat peanut oil in a small pot on medium heat and stir-fry shallots until just soft. Add ginger and chilli, continuing to stir until fragrant.

7. Mix soy and fish sauce, stock and palm sugar together, keeping 1 tablespoon aside to mix with the cornflour. Add to the pot and bring to the boil. Mix reserved sauce with cornflour and use to slightly thicken the sauce. Simmer for 3 minutes on a low–medium heat.

8. Just before serving, add whole basil leaves to wilt and then coriander.

9. To serve, place whole fish onto one large serving platter and pour over sauce.

Trevally baked in a citrus salt crust with mustard and tarragon aioli

SERVES 4 | Recipe by Mark Dronjak

This is a great way to cook whole trevally. The salt crust, infused with citrus zest, perfumes the fish and keeps it exceptionally moist.

MUSTARD AND TARRAGON AIOLI

2 tsp finely chopped fresh tarragon

1 tsp fresh lime juice

1 tsp fresh lime zest

Splash of tarragon vinegar

2 egg yolks

1 tsp creamy mustard

1 tsp hot English mustard (pre-prepared)

150–200ml extra virgin olive oil

Salt and freshly ground pepper

Caster sugar (optional)

300–500g whole trevally (or very fresh mullet), cleaned, gutted and scaled

500g rock salt

2 egg whites

Zest and juice of 1 lime

Zest and juice of 1 lemon

1. To make mustard and tarragon aioli, whisk together tarragon, lime juice and zest, vinegar, egg yolks and mustards.

2. Slowly drizzle in oil, while whisking, until the desired consistency is reached. Adjust seasoning to taste, adding a little sugar if aioli is too sharp. Store in the fridge until required.

3. Preheat oven to 200°C.

4. Place fish on a lightly greased oven tray.

5. Combine rock salt, egg whites and zests and adjust consistency as required to form a thick slurry. Pack rock salt slurry over fish, covering well.

6. Place fish in the oven and bake for 15–20 minutes. Remove fish from the oven. Crack open salt crust and remove, brushing any excess salt off fish with a pastry brush.

7. To serve, place fish on a platter and sprinkle with lime and lemon juice to taste. Serve with mustard and tarragon aioli and a good, crusty French bread.

Scallop and potato Panang curry

SERVES 4 | Recipe by Petra New

Potatoes carry flavour and are a cost-effective way to bulk out a recipe. Homemade curry pastes are super-quick to make and the fresh flavours really make all the difference. Make extra paste to keep in the freezer.

CURRY PASTE

1 tsp coriander seeds

½ tsp cumin seeds

1 cardamom pod

¼ tsp each salt and black peppercorns

1 long green chilli, deseeded (optional)

6 red chillies, dried, deseeded and soaked

2cm piece galangal, sliced

5cm lemongrass, sliced

4 Kaffir lime leaves, de-stemmed and torn

1 bunch fresh coriander, stems and roots, chopped

1 shallot, diced

2 cloves garlic, chopped

½ tsp shrimp paste

1 tbsp peanut oil

½ onion, diced

400g potatoes, peeled and cubed

200ml coconut milk

200ml coconut cream, reserving 1 tbsp for garnish

30ml fish sauce

1 tsp dark palm sugar

400g fresh scallops

¼ cup fresh basil leaves

1 tbsp lime juice

1 Kaffir lime leaf, finely shredded, for garnish

1. To make curry paste, place coriander seeds, cumin seeds and cardamom pod in a pan and dry-roast. Transfer to a mortar and pestle, add salt and black peppercorns and grind into a powder. Add remaining ingredients and pound to form a paste.

2. Heat oil in a pan on a medium heat and fry onion and curry paste for 2 minutes. Add potato and cook for another 2 minutes.

3. Reduce heat and add coconut milk and half of the coconut cream. Simmer for 10 minutes. Add fish sauce and palm sugar.

4. Test potato and when just cooked, add scallops, basil and remaining coconut cream. Cook for a few minutes, taking care not to overcook scallops. When scallops are just cooked, remove pan from the heat and squeeze in lime juice.

5. Serve curry in bowls, garnished with reserved coconut cream and shredded Kaffir lime leaf.

Smoked fish pies

SERVES 4 | Recipe by Jo Cooper and Harrison McIntyre

Classic potato-topped smoked fish pies.

MASHED POTATOES

900g Agria potatoes, peeled and cut
　　into chunks
¼–½ cup milk
60g butter
Salt and freshly ground pepper

WHITE SAUCE

70g butter
½ cup plain flour
½ tsp mustard powder
700ml milk
Salt and freshly ground pepper
Freshly grated nutmeg

Zest and juice of ½ lemon
2 tbsp chopped fresh chives
2 tbsp chopped fresh parsley
500g freshly smoked white fish, pulled off
　　the bone and broken into pieces

1. To make mashed potatoes, add potato to a medium-sized pot and just cover with cold water. Add approximately ½ teaspoon salt. Bring to the boil, then simmer until potatoes are cooked (soft when cut with a knife). Drain off water, then place the pot back on the heat to evaporate off any excess water. Remove from heat. Mash potatoes with a masher. Add milk and butter and fluff up with a fork. Season to taste.

2. Preheat oven to 200°C.

3. To make white sauce, melt butter in a pot and add flour. Stir over a gentle heat for 1 minute. Add mustard powder.

4. Gradually add milk, stirring constantly until a thick, smooth sauce is achieved (add more milk if too thick). Add seasoning and nutmeg. Leave to cool slightly.

5. Add lemon zest and juice, chopped herbs and smoked fish to the white sauce.

6. Place mixture into 4 ramekins (or a large shallow baking dish if you prefer a single pie) and top with mashed potato.

7. Bake for 15 minutes (or a bit longer if making a single pie) until sauce is bubbling and potato is golden on top.

Market fish with eggplant, tomato and mozzarella

SERVES 4 | Recipe by Mark Dronjak

This meal is Italian comfort food at its finest.

Olive oil
2 cloves garlic, finely chopped
400g can peeled Italian tomatoes, chopped
10 basil leaves, roughly torn
1 large whole eggplant, thinly sliced
200g mozzarella, sliced
50g Parmesan, freshly grated
Sea salt and freshly ground pepper
4 × 175g market-fresh fish fillets (e.g. red snapper, tuna, tarakihi, snapper or alfonsino)
Small handful of fresh aromatic herbs (e.g. oregano, parsley, chives and rosemary), stalks removed and finely chopped

1. Preheat oven to 180–200°C.

2. Heat a dash of olive oil in a pan and add garlic. Add tomatoes and half of the basil. Simmer for 5 minutes.

3. Place eggplant in a heated frying pan, adding a good dash of olive oil. Cook until golden brown on both sides. Place on a paper towel to drain off excess oil.

4. Spread a little tomato sauce in an oven dish to cover the bottom. Place eggplant slices in the dish with a little more tomato sauce and a slice of mozzarella on each. Sprinkle over remaining basil leaves and dust with Parmesan. Season to taste.

5. Toss fish fillets in herbs and place on top of eggplant.

6. Bake for 10–15 minutes or until fish is cooked.

Poached monkfish in potato and tomato casserole ▶

SERVES 4 | Recipe by John Campbell

Use any chunky white fish fillet to make a great hearty casserole. The addition of black or green olives towards the end gives a flavour twist.

300ml fish or vegetable stock (see fish stock recipe page 272)
600ml monkfish (or hapuku), cut into large chunks
2 tbsp extra virgin olive oil
1 onion, diced
4 cloves garlic, chopped
½ tsp paprika
Pinch of cayenne pepper
400g can chopped tomatoes
2 capsicums, sliced
400g Nadine potatoes, peeled and diced
Salt and freshly ground pepper
100ml white wine
50g good-quality black or green olives
Flat-leaf parsley, chopped, for garnish

1. Heat stock to boiling and poach fish in the stock for 2 minutes.

2. Heat a large casserole dish (or electric frying pan) with oil and cook onion and garlic for a few minutes until transparent, without colouring. Add spices, tomato, capsicum and potato. Season to taste.

3. Add wine and just cover with the poaching stock, then cook for approximately 15 minutes. Add fish and olives, and cook for another few minutes. Check seasoning.

4. Sprinkle with some flat-leaf parsley and serve from the casserole dish or a deep platter.

Baked market fish with white bean purée, fennel salad and orange oil

SERVES 4 | Recipe by Marco Edwardes

The citrus oil in this dish creates a refreshing lift.

WHITE BEAN PURÉE

60ml olive oil

2 shallots, thinly sliced

1 clove garlic, finely chopped

600g canned white beans, drained
  and rinsed

250ml chicken stock

Zest and juice of 1 lemon

Salt and freshly ground white pepper

ORANGE OIL

200ml orange juice

100ml grape seed oil

4 × 160g seasonal fish fillets

1 fennel bulb

1½ tbsp salted capers, rinsed

¼ cup torn flat-leaf parsley

1. Preheat oven to 200°C.

2. To make white bean puree, heat one-third of the olive oil in a pan over a low heat. Add shallots and garlic. Cook for 4–5 minutes, until tender.

3. Add white beans and chicken stock. Continue to cook until liquid has reduced by half and beans are warmed through, approximately 3–4 minutes.

4. Pulse mixture in a food processor until coarsely chopped. Return to the pan. Stir through half the lemon zest and juice. Season to taste and set aside to keep warm.

5. To make orange oil, heat orange juice in a pot until syrupy. Set aside to cool. Using a blender, slowly add grape seed oil to juice in a thin stream until emulsified.

6. Place fish on an oven tray lined with baking paper. Drizzle fish with half of the remaining olive oil and a little lemon juice. Roast until fish is cooked to your liking, 5–6 minutes for medium–rare.

7. Thinly slice fennel. Place in iced water until crisp, approximately 1–2 minutes. Remove and drain well.

8. Combine fennel in a bowl with capers and parsley. Add remaining olive oil, lemon zest and juice. Season to taste. Toss to combine.

9. Serve fish on top of white bean purée. Top with fennel salad and drizzle with orange oil.

Bengali-style fish curry

SERVES 4 | Recipe by Petra New

A healthy, light curry style. It's also great with prawns.

600g firm white fish (e.g. hapuku, monkfish or ling)

1 tbsp turmeric

1 tsp salt

CURRY PASTE

1 red chilli, deseeded (optional) and chopped

2 green chillies, deseeded (optional) and chopped

2cm piece fresh ginger, peeled and chopped

4 cloves garlic, chopped

1 tbsp whole mustard seeds, dry-roasted

2 onions, chopped

2 firm ripe tomatoes, chopped

Soy bean oil

1 tbsp mustard oil

¼ cup chopped fresh coriander

Salt and freshly ground pepper

4 cups freshly cooked Basmati rice, to serve

1. Dice fish into 2cm cubes. Sprinkle with turmeric and salt, mix and set aside.

2. To make curry paste, using a mortar and pestle grind chillies, ginger, garlic and mustard seeds. Remove and then grind onions and tomatoes. Mix both pastes together.

3. Add a splash of soy bean oil to a heated pan and seal fish on both sides. Remove fish from the pan.

4. Add mustard oil to the pan and fry off curry paste until aromatic. Add 1½ cups water and bring to the boil. Simmer for 5 minutes. Add fish to cook through. Fold in coriander and season to taste.

5. Serve curry with rice.

COOK'S NOTE

Try using leatherjacket in fish curries or stews. Leatherjacket is usually sold headed, gutted and skinned (then also known as cream fish). Simmer in the curry or stew for 4 minutes, then take off the heat and leave to rest for a further 2 minutes. Also try barbecued leatherjacket. De-head and gut the fish (or request your fishmonger to do this for you), brush with spice-infused olive oil and place on a medium–hot grill for 2 minutes each side. The thick skin will protect the flesh so that it stays juicy and moist.

Baked fish with Mediterranean crumble

SERVES 4 | Recipe by Petra New

This crumble is also very good on salmon or even used as a stuffing for lamb.

2 tomatoes

Olive oil

2 cloves garlic, crushed

½ red onion, diced

¼ preserved lemon (see recipe page 271), skin only, diced

¼ cup Kalamata olives, pitted and chopped

50g feta

3 tbsp each chopped fresh basil and parsley

1 slice bread, crumbed

4 × 200g seasonal white fish fillets

1. Bring a pot of water to the boil. Cross bottom of tomatoes with a knife. Place them in boiling water for 20 seconds, then plunge into iced water. Remove skin and seeds, then dice flesh.

2. Preheat oven to 220°C.

3. Heat a pan and add oil. Sauté garlic and onion until transparent and fragrant. Cool.

4. In a bowl, mix together diced tomato, garlic, onion, preserved lemon skin, olives, feta, herbs and breadcrumbs. Season to taste. Slowly add just enough olive oil to coat the topping.

5. Place one-quarter of mix on each fish fillet.

6. Bake for 8–10 minutes.

7. Serve with a tossed green salad and crunchy oven-baked bread.

Mussels steamed in Thai red curry with citrus ▶

SERVES 4 | Recipe by Steve Roberts

New Zealand mussels Asian-style. Beautiful Thai flavours that go well with an icy cold beer.

2 stalks lemongrass (thick bottom third only), bruised and halved lengthwise

2 Kaffir lime leaves, thinly sliced

3 tsp Thai red curry paste (see recipe page 271)

200ml coconut cream

2 tsp fish sauce

1 tbsp palm sugar

32 mussels, cleaned

1 spring onion, thinly sliced, for garnish

2 red chillies, deseeded (optional) and thinly sliced, for garnish

Handful of coriander, for garnish

1. Combine lemongrass, Kaffir lime leaves, curry paste, coconut cream, fish sauce and palm sugar in a bowl.

2. Place mussels in a lidded saucepan with curry mix. Cover and steam until opened, approximately 4 minutes.

3. To serve, transfer mussels to a serving bowl and pour over broth. Garnish with spring onion, chillies and coriander.

Baked white fish with Pernod cream sauce and potatoes

SERVES 4 | Recipe by John Campbell

A French twist, blending cream, butter, spinach and nutmeg with fresh seasonal white fish.

400g Nadine or new potatoes

1 iceberg lettuce

400g spinach

4 × 150g white fish fillets (e.g. snapper, tarakihi, hapuku)

250ml fish stock (see recipe page 272)

1 tbsp Pernod

300ml cream

40g butter

Salt and freshly ground pepper

1 nutmeg, for grating

1. Preheat oven to 180°C.

2. Peel and shape potatoes like little wine barrels.

3. Blanch four large lettuce leaves in boiling water for 2 minutes. Refresh in cold water, remove and dry off. Remove stalks from spinach, blanch and refresh. Squeeze moisture out of the leaves.

4. In a small pot, boil potatoes in water for 6–8 minutes. Remove when cooked.

5. Fold a piece of fish in a lettuce leaf and place in a reducing pan with about 100ml fish stock. Repeat to use all leaves and fish (without adding further stock to the pan). Bring to the boil and finish in the oven, covered, for 4–5 minutes. Remove fish parcels and keep warm.

6. Add most of the remaining stock to the pan and reduce by half. Add Pernod and cream and reduce by half again, then swish or shake in 25g of the butter. This will thicken the sauce and make it shine. Season to taste. Keep warm, but don't let it boil.

7. In a small pan, add a little of the remaining butter and a few spoons of stock and use this liquid to reheat potatoes (this will also make them shine).

8. Sauté spinach with remaining butter and grate in a little nutmeg. Season and place in a side bowl.

9. To serve, spoon sauce into a shallow bowl, top with the fish and garnish with potatoes. Serve spinach on the side.

Fish pie with puff pastry

SERVES 4 | Recipe by Colin Doyle

A luscious meal for the colder months, this pie combines the sweetness of parsnip and fennel with the smoky notes of smoked fish and the richness of salmon under a crispy, golden pastry dome. As an alternative, try omitting the pastry top and covering the pie with a rich mash of Agria potatoes, cream, butter and egg yolk.

60g butter

1 small carrot, finely diced

1 bulb fennel, finely diced

1 leek, finely diced

1 parsnip, finely diced

½ cup dry white wine

1 cup milk

½ cup cream

3 tbsp flour

Salt and freshly ground pepper

150g salmon

300g white fish (e.g. snapper, gurnard or tarakihi), diced

150g smoked white fish, diced

1 sheet puff pastry

1 egg yolk, beaten

1. Melt one-quarter of the butter in a pan over low heat and add diced carrot, fennel, leek and parsnip. Gently cook vegetables without allowing them to brown. Add wine and cook until wine is mostly absorbed. Add milk and cream, then set aside off the heat to allow milk and cream to warm through.

2. Melt remaining butter in a pan and add flour. Cook over a medium heat for approximately 2 minutes, until the flour lightens a couple of shades. Do not allow flour to burn. Strain liquid from vegetables and whisk it into flour. Cook until sauce thickens. Season to taste.

3. Preheat oven to 200°C.

4. Mix fish with sauce and cooked vegetables in a 23cm pie dish.

5. Place sheet of pastry over the pie plate and crimp around the edges with a fork. Cut several steam vents in the top and trim around the plate. Any off-cuts can be made into fish shapes to decorate the top of the pie. Brush pastry with egg yolk.

6. Place pie dish on the centre shelf of the oven for 10 minutes, then drop the temperature to 180°C for another 30 minutes or until the pastry is puffed and golden, and the filling is bubbling up through the vents.

Tea-steamed salmon with Thai red curry and coconut cream emulsion

SERVES 4 | Recipe by Steve Roberts

A wonderful Asian-inspired way to serve salmon.

150g jasmine tea leaves

5cm piece of ginger, finely sliced

4 spring onions, white parts only, roughly sliced

Good handful of fresh coriander roots

½ red chilli, deseeded (optional) and finely sliced

1 square of banana leaf

Salt and freshly ground pepper

4 × 180g salmon fillets (or hapuku, monkfish or kingfish) cut into neat squares

4 baby bok choy

Micro greens, for garnish

THAI RED CURRY AND COCONUT CREAM EMULSION

125ml fish stock (see recipe page 272)

1 tablespoon Thai red curry paste (see recipe page 271)

170ml coconut cream

Juice of 2 limes

1–2 tbsp fish sauce

1 tbsp shaved palm sugar

1. Add sufficient water to the bottom of a steamer. Add tea leaves, ginger, spring onion, coriander root and chilli.

2. Put the lid on the steamer and bring to the boil, then turn down to a simmer and allow the aromatics 4–5 minutes to infuse.

3. Line the top of the steamer with the banana leaf. Season salmon and baby bok choy and place in the steamer. Steam for around 5–7 minutes, then remove.

4. To make Thai red curry and coconut cream emulsion, add fish stock, curry paste and coconut cream to a pan and bring to the boil. Add lime juice, fish sauce and palm sugar. Stir and simmer for 1–2 minutes.

5. To serve, spoon some emulsion into the centre of 4 serving plates. Place a bok choy in the middle of each plate and top with salmon. Garnish with micro greens and swirl some more emulsion around the plate.

Soups, stocks and chowders

Seafood soup with garlic crostini   242

Oysters and salmon in Asian broth   244

Fish head soup   244

Moroccan fish ball soup   245

Thai hot and sour prawn soup   245

Japanese crayfish soup   246

Garlic and ginger sautéed fish with pumpkin soup   247

Fish consommé   248

Fish velouté   249

Pipi soup bach-style   249

Fish, tomato and lemongrass soup   250

Spicy scallop and noodle soup   250

Tuatua soup   252

Chenin Blanc nage with a seafood medley and summer vegetables   253

Mussel chowder   254

Seafood chowder   254

Crayfish bisque with leek and prawns   256

Bouillabaisse   257

Seafood soup with garlic crostini

SERVES 4 | Recipe by Marco Edwardes

This soup is full of goodness, making it ideal for the cooler winter days. Any combination of fish and shellfish will work.

GARLIC CROSTINI

100ml olive oil

2–3 cloves garlic, crushed

1 tbsp chopped parsley

Salt and freshly ground pepper

Day-old French stick

4 tbsp olive oil

4 tbsp finely diced onion

2 cups julienned leeks, carrots, fennel, courgette and celery

80g potatoes, peeled and diced (5mm)

Salt and freshly ground pepper

1 litre fish stock (see recipe page 272), scented with a pinch of saffron (optional)

100g salmon, diced

100g fresh white fish (e.g. tarakihi, gurnard or snapper), diced

200g cooked green-lipped mussels, shelled, foot and beard removed

8 raw prawn cutlets

8 cherry tomatoes, cut in half

Fresh herbs (chives, dill, parsley and chervil), finely chopped

1. Preheat oven to 180°C. Line an oven tray with baking paper.

2. To make garlic crostini, in a bowl mix together oil, garlic and parsley. Season to taste.

3. Cut French stick into thin slices. Place slices on the tray and brush with garlic oil.

4. Bake for approximately 5 minutes until golden brown.

5. Heat oil in a medium-sized pot and sauté onion, julienned vegetables and potato. Season to taste. Add fish stock and bring to the boil.

6. Add fish pieces, mussels, prawns and cherry tomatoes.

7. Let soup simmer for 3 minutes, then add chopped herbs. Season to taste.

8. Divide between 4 warm soup bowls and serve with warm garlic crostini.

Oysters and salmon in Asian broth

SERVES 4 | Recipe by Steve Roberts

A fantastically flavoured broth bursting with citrus flavours.

1 tbsp extra virgin olive oil

1 leek (white part only), finely sliced

3 Kaffir lime leaves

1 stalk lemongrass, cut in half and bruised

125ml white wine

1 litre fish stock (see recipe page 272)

1 sprig fresh thyme, leaves picked

4 × 100g salmon fillets

2 large ripe tomatoes, deseeded and diced

12 oyster mushrooms, sliced

16 Pacific rock oysters, removed from shell

1 bunch spinach leaves, washed and stems removed, leaves thinly sliced

Fresh coriander leaves, for garnish

1. Heat oil in a saucepan and gently cook leek, Kaffir lime leaves and lemongrass until soft, but not coloured.

2. Add wine and bring to a simmer. Reduce by two-thirds. Add fish stock and thyme and simmer for 2–3 minutes. Remove from heat and strain.

3. Either sear salmon in a pan or poach gently in the broth to cook.

4. To serve, add tomato, oyster mushrooms, oysters and spinach leaves to serving bowls and pour over hot broth. Garnish with coriander leaves.

Fish head soup

SERVES 4 | Recipe by Petra New

Use non-oily fish for this recipe to avoid an oil slick in your soup.

2 fish heads (e.g. snapper heads)

1 tbsp cracked pepper

2cm galangal (see glossary page 276), sliced

10cm lemongrass, bruised and split in half

1 spring onion, separated into white (bruised) and green (chopped)

⅓ pineapple, peeled and diced

200g canned bamboo shoots

2 tbsp fish sauce

¼ cup fresh chopped coriander

Juice of 1 lime

1. Split fish heads in half. Rub with pepper.

2. In a large pot bring 1.5 litres water to a rapid boil. Add galangal and lemongrass, and white part of spring onion. Add fish head halves and cook for 10 minutes.

3. Reduce heat and add pineapple and bamboo shoots. Cook for a further 5 minutes. Add fish sauce, green spring onion and coriander.

4. Remove from heat and squeeze in lime juice.

5. Ladle into bowls, making sure each person gets half of a head.

Moroccan fish ball soup

SERVES 4 | Recipe by Petra New

This tasty soup is scented to perfection.

500g inexpensive white fish, roughly chopped
1 onion, roughly chopped
¼ cup flat-leaf parsley, roughly chopped
1 slice bread, crust removed
100ml warm water
½ tsp cayenne pepper
1 tsp ground cumin
1 tsp ground coriander
Salt and freshly ground pepper
500ml fish stock (see recipe page 272)
1 carrot, finely diced
1 stalk celery, finely diced
Juice of ½ lemon
Flat-leaf parsley, chopped, for garnish

1. Place fish, onion and parsley in a blender and process until minced.

2. Soak bread in warm water until soggy. Squeeze out water, chop and add to fish mixture.

3. In a pan, dry-roast cumin and coriander. Add to fish mixture with the cayenne pepper, season and mix well. Wet your hands and shape mixture into balls.

4. Bring fish stock to the boil in a pan. Add carrot and celery. Cook for 5 minutes. Add fish balls, then bring soup back to the boil. Skim if necessary. Reduce heat and simmer for a further 10 minutes. Season to taste.

5. Ladle into bowls and top with a squeeze of lemon juice and a sprinkle of chopped parsley.

Thai hot and sour prawn soup

SERVES 4 | Recipe by Petra New

Chicken stock gives this soup a more rounded flavour without being 'too fishy'.

3 cups chicken stock
6 cloves garlic, crushed
6 shallots, sliced
2 stalks lemongrass, cut into 2cm lengths and bruised
2cm galangal root (see glossary page 276), thinly sliced
200g small button mushrooms
2 tomatoes, each cut into 8 wedges
3 large red chillies, deseeded (optional) and sliced
3 tbsp fish sauce
5 fresh Kaffir lime leaves, stems removed
300g raw shelled whole prawns
2–3 tbsp fresh lime juice
½ cup chopped fresh coriander, for garnish

1. In a pot bring chicken stock to the boil. Add garlic, shallots, lemongrass and galangal. Simmer for 3 minutes.

2. Add mushrooms and tomato and simmer for 2 minutes.

3. Add chillies, fish sauce, Kaffir lime leaves and prawns and simmer for 2 minutes.

4. Ladle into bowls, squeeze in lime juice and garnish with coriander.

Japanese crayfish soup

SERVES 4 AS A STARTER | Recipe by Steve Roberts

Savoury Japanese custard is considered more of a soup in Japanese cuisine and is found at many izakaya (Japanese-style pubs) and on the family table. A great starter or light lunch dish. The leftover dashi will keep in the fridge for 3 days, or you can freeze it.

DASHI STOCK

(MAKES ABOUT 1 LITRE)

10cm square of kombu (see glossary page 276)

1.5 litres water

20g katsuobushi (dried bonito flakes)

1 raw crayfish tail, meat cubed

3 tsp Kikkoman soy sauce

2 tsp mirin

2 tsp sake

Pinch of salt

4 eggs, very lightly beaten

4 fresh shiitake mushrooms, quartered

1 spring onion, sliced

1 tbsp pine nuts

1. To make dashi stock, wipe kombu with a damp cloth and cut into strips.

2. Place kombu in a pot with water and slowly bring to the boil. Quickly add 60ml more cold water to stop the boiling process.

3. Add bonito flakes and simmer for approximately 15 minutes.

4. Remove from heat and allow bonito flakes to sink to the bottom. Strain.

5. Bring approximately 625ml dashi to a boil. Add crayfish and simmer for approximately 30 seconds. Remove and allow to cool. Allow dashi to cool also.

6. Add soy sauce, mirin, sake and salt to dashi. Pour this mixture onto the eggs and mix very lightly so you don't create too many bubbles. Strain through a fine sieve.

7. Divide crayfish and remaining ingredients between 4 bowls and ladle in egg mix.

8. Place bowls into a steamer and steam for 8–12 minutes with a tea towel covering the steamer, until just set.

9. Serve with chopsticks to eat the solid pieces.

DID YOU KNOW?

Adult crayfish migrate to deeper waters, sometimes travelling 20 kilometres or more, to mate and lay their eggs.

Garlic and ginger sautéed fish with pumpkin soup

SERVES 4 | Recipe by Steve Roberts

Any fish will go well with this dish. For a touch of elegance, try serving it in demitasse cups.

PUMPKIN SOUP

20ml oil

1 tbsp Thai red curry paste (see recipe page 271)

1kg diced pumpkin, roasted until golden brown

500ml chicken or fish stock (see recipe page 272)

25g palm sugar

20ml fish sauce

500ml coconut cream

Salt and freshly ground pepper

400g white fish fillets, skinned and boned and cut into small chunks (or 24 raw prawn cutlets)

50ml olive oil

Small knob of ginger, finely chopped

2 cloves fresh garlic, finely chopped

3 Kaffir lime leaves, finely shredded, for garnish

1. To make pumpkin soup, gently heat oil in a pan. Add curry paste and sauté a little. Add pumpkin and stock and simmer for 10 minutes.

2. Purée in a blender, then pass through a fine sieve into a clean pan. Bring soup back to a simmer. Add palm sugar and fish sauce. Stir in coconut cream and check seasoning.

3. Sauté fish or prawns in olive oil with ginger and garlic until cooked through. Remove from heat.

4. Serve soup in bowls with fish or prawns arranged in the middle. Garnish with shredded Kaffir lime leaves.

DID YOU KNOW?

Gemfish are fast-swimming, voracious predators with strong jaws and knife-like teeth that should be avoided when handling the fish, either dead or alive.

Fish consommé

SERVES 4 | Recipe by John Campbell

Consommés are deceptive; they are not as difficult to make as you might think. You can use this consommé as a base for a spectacular terrine – impressive stuff for a dinner party. This consommé keeps for 2–3 days, or you can freeze it. I don't agree with the practice of adding ice to the mixture, as it dilutes the flavours.

CONSOMMÉ

1 carrot

1 onion

1 stalk celery

½ small leek (white part only)

1.5 litres fish stock (see recipe page 272), chilled

100g fish trimmings (offcuts)

1 tbsp tomato paste

1 clove garlic, chopped

2–3 stems dill or fennel

1 unwrapped bouquet garni (see glossary page 276)

3 egg whites

Salt and freshly ground pepper

100g white fish fillets, cut into strips

4 raw prawn cutlets

50ml sherry (optional)

1 tomato, diced, for garnish

4 spring onions, chopped, for garnish

Sprigs of chervil or dill, chopped, for garnish

1. To make consommé, wash, trim and peel vegetables. Process in a food processor until finely minced. Place in a large pan and add all remaining consommé ingredients, except for seasoning.

2. Set the pan over a medium heat and stir until the mixture is hot but not boiling. Stop stirring. The mixture should then form a solid mass of egg white on top.

3. Partially move the saucepan off the heat so the broth is just simmering for 1 hour. Do not let it boil or it will turn cloudy. Season lightly.

4. To strain, carefully ladle the consommé into a sieve lined with clean muslin or a damp coffee filter set over a jug or bowl.

5. Steam or poach fish fillets and prawns for a few minutes.

6. To serve, divide fish and prawns among 4 soup bowls. Pour in consommé and splash in a little sherry (if using). Garnish with tomato, spring onions and herbs. Serve immediately.

Fish velouté

MAKES APPROXIMATELY 1 LITRE
Recipe by John Campbell

A base sauce that can be flavoured to suit a number of fish dishes.

1.5 litres fish stock (see recipe page 272)
2 tbsp clarified butter
2 tbsp plain flour

1. Heat fish stock until hot (without boiling).

2. In a separate heavy-bottomed pan, melt clarified butter over a medium heat. Do not let it turn brown.

3. Using a wooden spoon, stir flour into melted butter, a little bit at a time, until it is fully incorporated. Heat paste for another minute or so to cook off the taste of raw flour, without browning.

4. Using a wire whisk, slowly add hot fish stock to the roux, whisking vigorously to make sure it's free of lumps.

5. Simmer for approximately 30 minutes or until the liquid reduces by approximately one-third, stirring frequently to ensure it does not stick. Use a ladle to skim off any impurities that rise to the surface. The sauce should be a velvety texture. If the sauce is too thick, add a little more hot stock.

6. Remove from the heat and strain.

Pipi soup bach-style

SERVES 4 | Recipe by John Campbell

This is gather-your-own-shellfish soup. It's equally good made with cockles, mussels or clams. See page 15 for instructions on purging sand from fresh shellfish.

2kg fresh pipi, purged
2 onions, chopped
4 cloves garlic, crushed
2 tbsp finely chopped parsley
100g bacon, diced
Freshly ground pepper
Fresh bread, to serve

1. Put pipi in a large lidded pan and barely cover with water. Add onion, garlic, parsley and bacon. Cover and boil rapidly for a few minutes. The soup is ready when all the pipi have opened.

2. Serve soup steaming hot with a touch of pepper and plenty of fresh bread.

DID YOU KNOW?
Maori harvesting pipi in the customary fashion often use flax baskets of a special design. The weave is open and allows smaller pipi to fall back on the bed as the gatherer swirls the basket through the water.

Fish, tomato and lemongrass soup

SERVES 4 | Recipe by Steve Roberts

A wonderfully light dish with so much flavour.

2 stalks lemongrass, bruised and roughly chopped
4 ripe tomatoes, chopped
2 shallots, diced
1 tbsp chopped fresh ginger
1 clove garlic, diced
1 red chilli, deseeded (optional) and roughly chopped
1.2 litres fresh fish stock (see recipe page 272)
2 tbsp fish sauce
1 tbsp finely julienned fresh ginger
2 tsp caster sugar
350g hapuku (or other white fish fillets), skinned and boned, cut into 2.5cm dice
1 extra tomato, deseeded and diced
1 Kaffir lime leaf, finely shredded
Small handful of chopped fresh coriander leaves
Small handful of chopped fresh basil leaves

1. Combine lemongrass, tomato, shallots, chopped ginger, garlic, chilli and fish stock and bring to the boil. Reduce to a simmer for around 20 minutes.

2. Strain and discard solids. Transfer broth to a clean pan.

3. Reheat and add fish sauce, ginger and sugar, followed by fish. Cook over a gentle heat for 3–4 minutes.

4. Divide diced tomato, Kaffir lime, coriander and basil leaves between serving bowls, ladle over soup and serve.

Spicy scallop and noodle soup ▶

SERVES 4 | Recipe by Petra New

This dish is also good with squid, mussels, prawns or white fish.

3 cups chicken stock
6 cloves garlic, crushed
6 shallots, sliced
2 stalks lemongrass, cut into 2cm lengths and bruised
2cm galangal root (see glossary page 276), sliced thinly
1½ large red chillies, deseeded (optional) and sliced
4 Kaffir lime leaves, torn into pieces
2 cups vermicelli rice noodles (pre-soaked)
200g small button mushrooms
3 tbsp fish sauce
24 scallops
Juice of 1 lime
¼ cup chopped fresh coriander
1 lime, cut into wedges, to serve

1. Heat stock. Add garlic, shallots, lemongrass, galangal, chilli and lime leaves. Gently simmer for 5 minutes to allow the flavours to infuse.

2. Add noodles, mushrooms and fish sauce. When mushrooms are cooked, turn up the heat and add scallops. Bring back to the boil and immediately turn off. Squeeze in lime juice and stir through coriander.

3. Ladle into bowls, making sure the scallops are evenly divided. Serve with wedges of lime.

Tuatua soup

SERVES 4 OR MORE | Recipe by John Campbell

If you are not able to source tuatua for this soup, replace them with pipi, cockles or mussels.

100g butter
1 small stalk celery, finely diced
½ carrot, finely diced
1 small leek, white part only, finely diced
½ onion, finely chopped
200g tuatua, shelled
1.5 litres fish stock (see recipe page 272)
1 bouquet garni (see glossary page 276)
⅓ cup short-grain rice
Freshly ground white pepper
2 spring onions, finely diced
½ cup cream, for garnish

1. Heat butter in a large pan and add vegetables. Cook gently for 4 minutes.

2. Chop tuatua (keep a little for garnishing) and add to vegetables. Add fish stock and bouquet garni and bring to the boil.

3. Add rice and cook for about 20 minutes or until rice is soft. Season to taste.

4. Remove bouquet garni. Blend soup in a food processor or liquidiser. Strain through a sieve.

5. Heat remaining tuatua in a pan with a little butter. Season and add spring onions.

6. Serve in heated bowls, topped with tuatua mixture and a swirl of cream.

Chenin Blanc nage with a seafood medley and summer vegetables

SERVES 4 | Recipe by Mark Dronjak

Chic, fancy and sophisticated.

500ml fish stock (see recipe page 272)

8 green king prawns, shell on (heads removed and used for stock)

200ml Chenin Blanc

12 cockles or clams, purged

8 green-lipped mussels, cleaned

1 medium–large carrot, cut into small dice

1 squid tube, sliced and scored

150g smoked salmon fillet, cut into medium pieces

12 scallops

400g firm-fleshed white fish fillets (e.g. hapuku, kingfish, monkfish or ling), skin on, scaled and diced

200g crème fraîche

75g asparagus spears, cut in half on an angle

6 chives, finely chopped

½ red capsicum, julienned

Sea salt and white pepper

30g butter

3 tbsp finely chopped parsley, for garnish

1. Heat fish stock in a large pan. Bring to a fast simmer. Add prawn heads and reduce liquid by a third. When reduced, add wine, cockles or clams and mussels. Cook until shells open, remove from pan and keep to one side. Discard any shellfish that do not fully open along with prawn heads.

2. Add carrot to the pan. Cook for 2–3 minutes. Add remainder of the seafood and simmer until cooked. Add crème fraîche, asparagus, chives and capsicum. Adjust seasoning. Add butter and check seasoning.

3. Serve in warmed bowls, garnished with parsley.

DID YOU KNOW?
Ling is one of New Zealand's top ten export earners for seafood. Its large, boned-out fillets and thick steaks hold their shape well in cooking and have proved to be popular at home and in commercial kitchens.

Mussel chowder

SERVES 4–6 | Recipe by John Campbell

The peppery taste of the horopito makes a great addition to the chowder. You could also use kawakawa in this dish.

20g butter
100g bacon, diced
1 onion, diced
2 cloves garlic, finely chopped
100g each of celery and leek, diced
100ml white wine
1 litre chicken stock
1 bouquet garni (see glossary page 276)
200g yellow kumara, diced
2 tsp horopito (see glossary page 276)
16 mussels, cleaned
200g watercress
Salt and freshly ground pepper
50ml cream (optional)
Fresh chives, chopped, for garnish
Smoked sea salt

1. Heat a good-sized pan and add butter. Gently fry bacon. Add onion, garlic, celery and leek. Cook over a low heat without colouring. Add wine and reduce a little.

2. Add stock, bouquet garni, kumara and horopito. Bring to the boil and simmer for 15 minutes. Add mussels and watercress. Bring back to the boil and simmer for a further 3 minutes. Season to taste.

3. Add cream (if using) and serve garnished with chives, smoked sea salt and fresh crusty bread on the side.

Seafood chowder ▶

SERVES 4 | Recipe by John Campbell

A classic chowder brimming with seafood.

20g butter
100g bacon, diced
1 onion, diced
2 cloves garlic, chopped
100g celery, diced
100ml white wine
1 litre chicken or fish stock (see recipe page 272)
1 bouquet garni (see glossary page 276) or 1 tbsp savoury herbs
200g potatoes, diced
12 each of mussels (half meat only, half in the shell) and prawns (meat only)
100g seafood marinara mixture (thawed)
120g seasonal white fish, cubed
Sea salt and freshly ground pepper
2 tbsp crème fraîche (optional)
Chopped fresh chives, for garnish

1. Heat a good-sized pan and add butter. Gently fry bacon. Add onion and garlic. Add celery and cook gently without colouring for a further few minutes.

2. Add wine. Reduce, then add stock, bouquet garni and potato. Bring to the boil and simmer for 15 minutes.

3. Add all seafood. Bring to the boil and simmer for 3 minutes. Season to taste and add crème fraîche (if using).

4. Serve in warmed soup bowls garnished with chives with crusty bread alongside.

Crayfish bisque with leek and prawns

SERVES 4 | Recipe by Marco Edwardes

Tasty, comforting and bursting with flavour.

1kg crayfish bodies
50ml olive oil
1 onion, finely chopped
2 cloves garlic, finely chopped
1 stalk celery, finely chopped
1 carrot, finely chopped
2 tbsp tomato paste
Splash of brandy
250ml white wine
1 litre fish stock (see recipe page 272)
Zest and juice of 1 lemon
Good pinch of saffron
500ml cream
1 sprig thyme
Salt and freshly ground pepper
½ small leek
8 raw prawns (meat, no tails)
Salt and freshly ground pepper

1. Bring a large pot of water to the boil and add crayfish bodies. Simmer for 2 minutes, then strain.

2. Heat another large pot. Add olive oil, onion, garlic, celery and carrot.

3. Add blanched crayfish bodies and tomato paste. Lightly fry for a few minutes.

4. Add brandy, wine and fish stock and bring to the boil. Add lemon zest and juice, saffron, cream and thyme. Season lightly and simmer for 20 minutes.

5. Strain bisque through a sieve into another pot and return to stovetop. Simmer bisque for a few more minutes while you cut leek into fine strips.

6. Heat a little olive oil in a small saucepan. Add leek and prawn meat and sauté until the leek is soft. Season to taste.

7. Serve bisque in warmed soup bowls garnished with leek and prawns.

Bouillabaisse

SERVES 4 | Recipe by Petra New

This is one stew where you want the seafood to hold its shape, so remember to watch the cooking phase carefully as seafood generally cooks quickly. Don't be afraid to remove pieces from the heat if necessary.

AIOLI
(MAKES 1 CUP)
3 cloves garlic
2 egg yolks
1 tsp Dijon mustard
Juice of 1 lemon
200ml soya or canola oil
Salt and white pepper

Extra virgin olive oil
1 onion, finely diced
½ leek, sliced
1 stalk celery, sliced
½ fennel bulb, sliced
1 large potato, cut into small dice
2 tomatoes
3 cloves garlic, crushed
2 bay leaves
Pinch of saffron, steeped in 1 tbsp
    warm water
½ orange, peel only
500ml fish stock (see recipe page 272)
Salt and freshly ground pepper
8 baby octopus
100g monkfish, cut into large dice
100g mullet, cut into large dice
100g salmon, cut into large dice
8 each of mussels, cleaned, pipi, purged
    and prawns, whole

1. To make aioli, crush garlic using a mortar and pestle until smooth.

2. In a clean bowl, whisk together garlic, egg yolks, mustard and lemon juice until it has lightened in colour. Start drizzling in oil extremely slowly so as not to 'split' the aioli (see Cook's Note page 189), while continuously whisking. When all the oil is in, taste and season. To make a creamy, less thick consistency, whisk in 1–2 tablespoons warm water.

3. Heat oil in a large pan. Cook onion until transparent. Add leek, celery, fennel and potato and cook without colouring for 3–5 minutes.

4. Cut tomatoes in half, squeeze out seeds and discard. Roughly chop flesh. Add to the pan along with garlic, bay leaves, saffron and orange peel. Allow a few minutes for these flavours to infuse, then add stock and bring to the boil. Season and simmer for 3 minutes.

5. Add baby octopus. When liquid is again simmering, add fish and shellfish.

6. When shellfish have opened ladle all the fish and vegetables into 4 bowls. Check and adjust seasoning of the broth and then ladle this over the seafood.

7. Serve with crusty bread and aioli.

Basic recipes

COATINGS

Yeast batter   260

Dukkah   260

Flour and egg battered fish   261

Chermoula   261

Crumbed fish   261

Cajun spice mix   261

DRESSINGS AND SAUCES

Basic vinaigrette   262

Honey and ginger vinaigrette   262

Warm tomato vinaigrette   262

Dill dressing   262

Spinach yoghurt dressing   263

Caesar dressing   263

Citrus and palm sugar dressing   263

Spicy yoghurt and harissa dressing   263

Lime glaze   264

Orange Pernod glaze   264

Seafood marinade   264

Vincotto reduction   264

Sauce remoulade   264

Mayonnaise   265

Paprika and red pepper mayonnaise   265

Garlic mayonnaise   265

Hollandaise   265

Sauce tartare   266

Salsa al pomodoro (tomato sauce)   266

Nuoc cham dipping sauce   266

Teppanyaki dipping sauce   266

Chilli sauce   267

SALSAS AND PESTOS

Tomato and basil salsa   268

Green salsa   268

Olive salsa   268

Macadamia and rocket pesto   269

Basil pesto   269

FLAVOURED BUTTERS

Dill butter   270

Garlic and herb butter   270

Lime and peppercorn butter   270

Pimento and chive butter   270

Tarragon butter   270

Tartare butter   270

Dried tomato and basil butter   270

Olive butter   270

OTHER ESSENTIALS

Preserved lemons   271

Thai red curry paste (nam prik gaeng phed)   271

Grilled citrus   271

Corn tortillas   272

Fresh egg pasta dough   272

Fish stock   272

Coatings

When preparing to coat fish, make sure the fish is dry and fully covered with the coating before cooking. Cook in a vegetable oil that does not have a strong flavour, e.g. canola or sunflower. You can also add a tablespoon of butter at the end of cooking for added flavour. Take care not to burn the butter, as this will affect the flavour of the fish.

Yeast batter

MAKES 1 LITRE (ENOUGH TO COAT APPROXIMATELY 10–12 FISH FILLETS)

Recipe by John Campbell

600ml milk
½ tbsp dry yeast
Pinch of sugar
300g plain flour
Salt

1. Heat milk in a pan until warm. Add yeast and sugar.

2. Sift flour into a bowl and make a well in the centre. Pour in milk mixture and leave until it forms small bubbles. Mix well and add a few pinches of salt.

3. Leave in a warm place. When batter puffs up it's ready to use.

COOK'S NOTE

This batter is light, crisp and good for shellfish, most white fish and for vegetables, too. As a variation, add 1 tablespoon green peppercorns, 2 teaspoons savoury herbs and 2 cloves of garlic to batter base.

Dukkah

MAKES APPROXIMATELY 150G (ENOUGH TO COAT APPROXIMATELY 4–6 FISH FILLETS)

Recipe by John Campbell

1 tbsp coriander seeds
1½ tsp cumin seeds
85g whole blanched almonds, toasted
½ tsp fennel seeds
55g sesame seeds
1 tsp ground cumin
½ tsp flaky sea salt
½ tsp ground black peppercorns

1. Place all ingredients over medium heat in a frying pan. Stir for approximately 2–3 minutes, until lightly toasted. Cool.

2. Place all ingredients into a food processor and process until a light crumb consistency is achieved.

COOK'S NOTE

This is great to use as a coating for fish fillets.

Flour and egg battered fish

YIELD ADAPTABLE | Recipe by Jo Cooper

Fish fillet
Seasoned plain flour
Lightly beaten egg

Dust dry fish fillet with flour and dip into beaten egg. Pan fry, turning once.

Chermoula

MAKES ½ CUP | Recipe by John Campbell

2 cloves garlic
1 tsp coarse salt
2 tsp ground cumin
1 tsp paprika
½ tsp cayenne pepper
Juice of 1 lemon
Small handful parsley and coriander, roughly chopped
3 tbsp olive oil

Using a mortar and pestle or food processor, pound garlic and salt to a smooth paste. Add cumin, paprika, cayenne pepper, lemon juice and coriander. Gradually add olive oil while pounding and stirring.

COOK'S NOTE
Rub chermoula over fish fillets or chunks as a marinade prior to cooking.

Crumbed fish

YIELD ADAPTABLE | Recipe by Jo Cooper

Fish fillet
Seasoned plain flour
Beaten egg
Breadcrumbs

Dust dry fish fillet with flour. Dip in egg and coat with breadcrumbs, ensuring fish is fully covered. Pan-fry, turning once.

Cajun spice mix

MAKES 1¼ CUPS | Recipe by Mark Dronjak

¼ cup salt
¼ cup cayenne pepper
¼ cup paprika
¼ cup garlic granules
¼ cup ground black pepper
2 tbsp onion granules
2 tbsp dried oregano
2 tbsp dried thyme

Mix all ingredients using a mortar and pestle. Store in an airtight container in a cool, dark place.

Dressings and sauces

Basic vinaigrette

MAKES 300ML | Recipe by John Campbell

50ml white vinegar
1 tbsp sugar or runny honey
1 tsp Dijon or mild mustard
Salt and freshly ground pepper
250ml olive oil and vegetable oil mix
 (sunflower or canola)

Whisk together vinegar, sugar or honey, mustard and seasoning in a bowl. Slowly blend in oils.

COOK'S NOTE
Replace the white vinegar with balsamic vinegar to create a balsamic vinaigrette.

Honey and ginger vinaigrette

MAKES 300ML | Recipe by John Campbell

1 tbsp runny honey (if sugar used in the basic
 vinaigrette, otherwise leave out)
1 tsp chopped fresh ginger
1 clove garlic, crushed
300ml basic vinaigrette (see recipe above)

Add honey, ginger and garlic to the basic vinaigrette.

Warm tomato vinaigrette

MAKES 300ML | Recipe by John Campbell

¾ cup olive oil
1 medium onion, diced
1 clove garlic, crushed
75ml white wine vinegar
50ml honey
1 tbsp tomato paste
400g can whole peeled tomatoes, roughly chopped
Salt and freshly ground pepper

1. Put oil in a small pan with onion and garlic and set over a moderate heat. Cover and cook gently for 2 minutes. Add remaining ingredients, except seasoning, and bring to the boil. Simmer for 5 minutes.

2. Blend in a food processor or liquidiser. Add seasoning to taste and serve with fish of your choice.

COOK'S NOTE
This simple sauce is great with deep-fried fish, grilled fish or pan-fried fish. If it is kept warm, it will not separate; if it does separate, give it a quick blend.

Dill dressing

MAKES 300ML | Recipe by John Campbell

1¼ cups sour cream
4 tsp chopped fresh dill
Juice of 1 lemon
1 tsp horseradish cream

Mix all ingredients together in a bowl.

Spinach yoghurt dressing

MAKES 500ML | Recipe by John Campbell

180g spinach, washed and trimmed
200ml plain unsweetened yoghurt
50ml each cream and milk, mixed together
Salt and freshly ground pepper

1. Blanch spinach in plenty of boiling salted water. Drain, refresh with cold water, squeeze and chop.
2. Put spinach and yoghurt in a blender and process until smooth. Add cream and milk to thin the dressing. Season lightly and strain. Mix all ingredients together in a bowl and use within 4 hours.

Caesar dressing

MAKES 500ML | Recipe by John Campbell

½ cup vinegar
1 egg
4 cloves garlic, chopped
4 anchovy fillets
1 tbsp mild Dijon or smooth mustard
Juice of 1 lemon
1½ cups olive oil, slightly warmed
Salt and freshly ground pepper

Put all ingredients, except oil and seasoning, in a food processor or liquidiser. Blend together, then slowly add oil. Season to taste.

Citrus and palm sugar dressing

MAKES 200ML | Recipe by John Campbell

Juice of 2 limes
Juice of 1 lemon
2 tbsp palm sugar, broken up
1 tsp fish sauce
1 tbsp sesame oil

Add all ingredients to a small bowl. Whisk together until palm sugar dissolves.

Spicy yoghurt and harissa dressing

MAKES 500ML | Recipe by Mark Dronjak

4 tbsp olive oil
1 clove garlic, peeled and crushed
2 tbsp chopped fresh coriander
2 cups plain unsweetened yogurt
Juice of 1 lemon
1–2 tsp dried red chilli, crushed
2 tsp cumin powder
Pinch of salt
1 tsp paprika
3 tsp caster sugar

Mix together all ingredients in a food processor or blender until sugar is dissolved. Refrigerate and serve alongside freshly cooked fish fillets.

Lime glaze

MAKES 250ML | Recipe by John Campbell

Juice of 8 limes
Juice of 2 lemons
100ml dry white wine
100ml water
100g sugar
1 tbsp arrowroot

Put all ingredients, except arrowroot, in a pan and bring to the boil. Mix arrowroot with a little water and add to lime mixture. Simmer for 2 minutes until mixture reaches the consistency of cream. Do not overcook. Strain glaze. Serve warm or at room temperature.

COOK'S NOTE
This glaze is superb with the whitebait flan (see recipe page 74). Also great with grilled fish sprinkled with Worcestershire sauce. If limes are not readily available, use lemons instead.

Orange Pernod glaze

MAKES 500ML | Recipe by Steve Roberts

400ml fresh orange juice
3 tbsp Pernod
50g unsalted butter, diced
Salt and freshly ground pepper

1. To a warm saucepan, add orange juice and Pernod. Reduce by two-thirds.
2. Slowly whisk in butter, one cube at a time. Season and keep warm until ready to use.

Seafood marinade

MAKES 50ML | Recipe by Steve Roberts

2 cloves garlic, peeled and finely chopped
2 Kaffir lime leaves, finely shredded
1 tbsp sweet Thai chilli sauce
2 tbsp kecap manis
Salt and freshly ground black pepper
1 tbsp chopped fresh coriander leaves

Combine all ingredients in a glass bowl.

Vincotto reduction

MAKES 150ML | Recipe by Steve Roberts

250ml fig vincotto
1 tbsp port
10g caster sugar

Use a heavy-bottomed saucepan over a very gentle heat to reduce by two-thirds. Leave to cool.

COOK'S NOTE
This goes well with everything from seafood to ice cream.

Sauce remoulade

MAKES 400ML | Recipe by John Campbell

1¼ cups sauce tartare (see recipe page 266)
1 tsp chopped fresh tarragon
1 tsp chopped fresh chervil
2 anchovy fillets, finely chopped

Mix all ingredients together in a bowl.

Mayonnaise

MAKES 300ML | Recipe by John Campbell

3 egg yolks
2 tbsp white vinegar
2 tsp lemon juice
1 tsp mild mustard
½ cup olive oil and 1 cup vegetable oil (e.g. canola, corn or sunflower), mixed together
Salt and white pepper

Put yolks in a bowl and whisk. Add vinegar, lemon juice and mustard. Very slowly drizzle in oil and continue whisking until thick. Season to taste.

Paprika and red pepper mayonnaise

MAKES 150ML | Recipe by Mark Dronjak

1½ tsp good Spanish paprika powder
1 egg yolk
1 tbsp white vinegar
1 tsp creamy mustard (e.g. Dijon)
2 tbsp finely chopped roasted red pepper (freshly roasted or preserved)
Salt and white pepper
100ml good light vegetable oil
1 tbsp olive oil

Whisk all ingredients together except oils. Drizzle oil in very slowly while whisking. Continue until combined and mayonnaise has thickened.

Garlic mayonnaise

MAKES 400ML | Recipe by John Campbell

1¼ cups fresh mayonnaise (see recipe left)
2½ tsp tomato paste
2 cloves garlic, peeled and finely crushed
½ tsp turmeric
1 tsp finely chopped fresh thyme
1 tsp finely chopped fresh parsley
Salt and freshly ground pepper

Mix all ingredients together in a bowl.

Hollandaise

MAKES 300ML | Recipe by John Campbell

300g unsalted butter
50ml dry white wine
2 tbsp white vinegar
4 egg yolks
Pinch of cayenne pepper
White pepper

1. Melt butter in a bowl over a pan of simmering water (or in the microwave). Leave to sit for 15 minutes. The milky residue will settle on the bottom. Do not boil, as the milky residue will stick.

2. Put wine and vinegar in a round-bottomed stainless steel bowl and mix in egg yolks. Place the bowl over a double boiler for approximately 5 minutes, stirring until yolks thicken. Slowly start adding butter, whisking all the time. When all butter is mixed in (discard any milky residue), the consistency should be that of half-whipped cream. Season with peppers. Keep warm until required.

Sauce tartare

MAKES 500ML | Recipe by John Campbell

1¼ cups mayonnaise (see recipe page 265)
50g gherkins, chopped
50g capers, chopped
2 tbsp chopped fresh parsley
Salt and freshly ground pepper (optional)

Mix all ingredients together in a bowl.

Salsa al pomodoro (tomato sauce)

MAKES 500ML | Recipe by Steve Roberts

400g can Italian tomatoes in juice
2 tbsp olive oil
½ small onion, finely chopped
2 cloves garlic, crushed
½ stalk celery, chopped
1 tbsp tomato purée
Salt and freshly ground pepper
¼–½ tsp sugar

1. In a food processor, purèe tomatoes in their juice.

2. In a saucepan, heat oil and gently cook onion, garlic and celery until translucent, without colouring.

3. Add puréed tomatoes and all remaining ingredients and simmer for approximately 15–20 minutes.

4. Process sauce again and strain. Check seasoning and adjust to taste.

COOK'S NOTE
This tomato sauce is perfect for seafood pasta dishes.

Nuoc cham dipping sauce

MAKES 500ML | Recipe by Steve Roberts

2 cloves garlic, peeled and minced
2 small fresh red chillies, deseeded and finely sliced
4 tbsp sugar
Juice of 3 limes (about ½ cup)
3 tbsp water
1 stalk lemongrass, finely chopped
½ cup fish sauce

Combine all ingredients in a bowl. Mix until sugar dissolves.

Teppanyaki dipping sauce

MAKES 200ML | Recipe by Steve Roberts

125ml soy sauce
65ml mirin or dry sherry
3 tsp sugar
1 tsp fresh ginger, peeled and finely grated

Combine all ingredients in a bowl. Mix until sugar dissolves.

COOK'S NOTE
This dipping sauce is great with a selection of grilled vegetables and seafood.

Chilli sauce

MAKES 400ML | Recipe by John Campbell

2 tbsp brown or palm sugar

2 tbsp soy sauce

2 tbsp water

1 tbsp sesame oil

¾ cup finely diced different-coloured capsicums

½ onion, finely diced

½ carrot, finely diced

1 small stalk celery, finely diced

3 cloves garlic, chopped

4 chillies, deseeded and chopped

1 bay leaf

1¼ cups stock made from a stock cube, or consommé

1 tbsp runny honey

2½ tsp chopped parsley

2 spring onions, thinly sliced

Freshly ground pepper

2 tbsp arrowroot (or cornflour)

1. Put sugar in a pan and set over high heat. Stir constantly until it melts and browns. Remove from heat and add soy sauce and water. Stand clear; the caramel is very hot and tends to spit when liquid is added.

2. Put oil in another pan and set over a moderate heat. Add vegetables, garlic and chilli. Cook gently for 4 minutes.

3. Add bay leaf, stock or consommé and honey. Cook gently for 15 minutes. Add parsley and spring onions. Season with pepper. Add caramel mix.

4. Mix arrowroot (or cornflour) with a little water and add to the sauce (add a little at a time to ensure it does not over-thicken; add a little water if it does). Cook for 2–3 minutes more until the sauce has thickened slightly.

COOK'S NOTE

This sauce goes well with hot or cold fish of all types. Alternatively, it can be used as a dressing, hot or cold.

Salsas and pestos

Tomato and basil salsa

MAKES 400ML | Recipe by John Campbell

3 cloves garlic, peeled and chopped
1 onion, diced
50ml olive oil
400g can whole skinned tomatoes, drained
   (reserve juice)
2 chillies, deseeded and finely chopped
2 spring onions, sliced
50ml white wine vinegar
12 fresh basil leaves
Salt and freshly ground pepper

1. In a wide, deep pan on a medium heat,
    gently cook garlic and onion in olive oil for
    3 minutes.

2. Chop tomatoes roughly and add them to
    the pan along with remaining ingredients,
    except seasoning.

3. Cook mixture for 10–15 minutes, until it
    is well reduced. Season to taste. If it's a little
    thick, add some of the reserved tomato juice.

COOK'S NOTE
*Serve this salsa either warm or at room temperature with
peppered, chargrilled or deep-fried fish.*

Green salsa

MAKES 300ML | Recipe by John Campbell

½ cup chopped fresh parsley
2 tbsp capers, drained
4 cloves garlic, crushed
3 anchovy fillets
½ cup fresh white breadcrumbs
4 tbsp olive oil
4 tbsp red wine vinegar
1 green capsicum, chopped
½ cup green olives, pitted and chopped
Salt and freshly ground pepper

Put all ingredients together in a food processor
and blend. Check and adjust seasoning if required.

Olive salsa

MAKES 300ML | Recipe by John Campbell

1 onion, diced
3 cloves garlic, peeled and crushed
60ml olive oil
100g each black and green olives, pitted and diced
100g tomato, diced
2 tbsp red wine vinegar
Salt and freshly ground pepper

Cook onion and garlic in olive oil gently for
3 minutes. Remove from heat and add the
remaining ingredients. Season to taste.

COOK'S NOTE
Serve warm with grilled, pan-fried or deep-fried fish.

Macadamia and rocket pesto

MAKES 300G | Recipe by Mark Dronjak

1 clove garlic, peeled and chopped
½ cup macadamia nuts, roughly chopped
1 cup fresh rocket leaves
Juice of 1 lemon
Olive oil
Salt and freshly ground pepper

1. Put garlic, macadamia nuts, rocket and lemon juice into a food processor. Add a good lug of olive oil and process until a smooth consistency – with little flecks of nuts in it – is reached.

2. Adjust seasoning. Add more oil as desired for consistency. Allow to rest before serving.

Basil pesto

MAKES 300G | Recipe by John Campbell

150g pine nuts
2 cups loosely packed fresh basil leaves
2 cloves garlic, peeled and chopped
50g Parmesan, grated
Salt and freshly ground pepper
50ml olive oil

1. Put pine nuts, basil, garlic and Parmesan in the food processor or blender and process until smooth. Season as required.

2. With the machine going, slowly pour in the oil.

3. If storing the pesto for later use, transfer to a container and pour a little oil over the top. Store refrigerated.

Flavoured butters

Flavoured butters keep well in the freezer. Always use soft butter and either whip for a few minutes in the food processor or beat with an electric beater before mixing in the rest of the ingredients. Serve on top of steamed or pan-fried fish.

ALL MAKE 500G | Recipes by John Campbell

Dill butter

Mix together 500g butter, 2 tablespoons chopped fresh dill and juice of 2 lemons.

Garlic and herb butter

Mix together 500g butter, 2 tablespoons chopped fresh mixed herbs (e.g. thyme, sage and chives), 2 cloves chopped garlic and 1 tablespoon Worcestershire sauce.

Lime and peppercorn butter

Mix together 500g butter, zest and juice of 4 limes and 2 tablespoons drained green peppercorns.

Pimento and chive butter

Mix together 500g butter, 20 finely cut fresh chives, 75g canned pimento and 2 tablespoons paprika.

Tarragon butter

Mix together 500g butter, 2 tablespoons chopped fresh tarragon and juice of 2 lemons.

Tartare butter

Mix together 500g butter, 2 tablespoons chopped parsley, 1 tablespoon chopped capers, 2 tablespoons chopped gherkins and juice of 2 lemons.

Dried tomato and basil butter

Mix together 500g butter, 20 torn fresh basil leaves and 50g chopped dried tomatoes.

Olive butter

Mix together 500g butter, 20 large pitted and chopped olives, 2 tablespoons chopped fresh parsley and 6 chopped anchovy fillets.

Other essentials

Preserved lemons

MAKES 1 JAR | Recipe by John Campbell

Good-quality lemons (quantity dependent on the
    jar size)
Rock salt
Cinnamon stick, bay leaf, coriander seeds (optional)
Lemon juice to cover

1. Clean and sterilise a jar.

2. Give lemons a good clean and cut off
   hard end bits. Cut lemons into quarters
   lengthwise, but don't cut all the way
   through. Rub quite a bit of rock salt into the
   cut lemons.

3. Sprinkle a little salt in the bottom of the
   sterilised jar. Place lemons in the jar, giving
   them a good squeeze while doing so. Add a
   little spice (if using). Cover with extra lemon
   juice and seal.

4. Leave for 1 month in a cool place (not
   the fridge), turning from time to time.
   When ready to use, lemons should be soft.
   Refrigerate after opening; they will last for
   months in the fridge.

COOK'S NOTE
If you prefer a less salty flavour, rinse lemons before using.

Thai red curry paste (nam prik gaeng phed)

MAKES 8 TABLESPOONS | Recipe by Petra New

1 tbsp coriander seeds, roasted
2 cardamom pods, roasted
½ tsp each black peppercorns and salt
10 large dried chillies, deseeded and soaked
5cm piece galangal, chopped
½ stalk lemongrass, chopped
6 Kaffir lime leaves, chopped
2 coriander roots (stalk and root only), chopped
1 shallot, chopped
4 cloves garlic, chopped
1 tsp shrimp paste
6 large fresh red chillies, deseeded (optional)
    and chopped

Grind coriander seeds, cardamom pods, pepper–
corns and salt into a powder using a mortar and
pestle. Add remaining ingredients and pound
until it forms a smooth paste.

Grilled citrus

MAKES 2 HALVES | Recipe by Colin Doyle

1 lemon or lime, cut in half
1 tbsp caster sugar

Dip cut face of lemon or lime in sugar and place
cut side down in a dry (no oil) pan. Allow sugar to
caramelise. You can omit the sugar if you prefer.

Corn tortillas

MAKES 12 | Recipe by Colin Doyle

2 cups instant corn masa mix (masa harina)
1 cup lukewarm water

1. In a medium-sized bowl, mix the masa harina with water. Mix for a couple of minutes until a soft, slightly tacky dough is formed. If the dough is dry, add a teaspoon of water at a time until the desired texture is achieved.

2. Divide dough into quarters, then divide each quarter into thirds to make 12 small balls. Cover with a damp tea towel to prevent drying out.

3. Place a ball of dough between two sheets of cling film and, using a rolling pin (or a tortilla press), shape each ball to a 150mm-diameter disc. Peel off the cling film.

4. Toast tortillas one at a time in a dry pan over medium heat for about 30 seconds. Turn and cook for another 45 seconds until the odd brown spot appears. Stack tortillas on a plate under a tea towel to prevent them drying out while the rest of the tortillas cook.

COOK'S NOTE

To make tortilla chips, press the masa dough thinner. When toasted, cut to the desired shape and deep-fry.

Fresh egg pasta dough

MAKES 500G | Recipe by Steve Roberts

500g '00' flour (if you can't source this, plain flour will do just as well)
5 eggs
Good pinch of salt
50ml olive oil

In a bowl, place sifted flour in a mound and make a well in the centre. Place eggs, salt and oil into the well. Mix to a dough. Tip out onto a lightly floured surface and knead for 10 minutes. Cover well with cling film. Place in the fridge for half an hour to rest until ready to shape and use.

Fish stock

MAKES 1.5 LITRES | Recipe by John Campbell

1 medium onion, sliced
1.5kg white fish bones, washed
2 litres cold water
Juice of 1 lemon
6 white peppercorns
1 bay leaf
2–3 stalks parsley

1. Place onion and fish bones into a large pot with cold water. Add lemon juice, peppercorns, bay leaf and parsley stalks. Bring to the boil, then turn down to simmer gently for 20 minutes. Remove the 'scum' by skimming off the top of the stock.

3. Strain immediately, leave to cool then cover and either refrigerate or freeze.

Contributing chefs

John Campbell trained in New Zealand before travelling to Sydney and through Asia, surfing whenever there were waves. He landed in London and worked in restaurants and hotels while gaining a certificate in Advanced Cookery at Westminster Catering College. Back in New Zealand, John opened The Penguin and a number of other restaurants followed. He has since held a variety of senior chef roles in Auckland and Wellington and was executive chef for the America's Cup in 2000. John's cookbook *Fast Fish, Fancy Fish* was published in 1993. He now owns and operates Squid, a catering company, and enjoys the flexibility of his cooking and teaching. **squidsquid@xtra.co.nz**

Cooking has always been a passion for self-taught Australian cook **Colin Doyle**. When he arrived in New Zealand from the United States nine years ago, having just completed a PhD in X-ray spectroscopy, he decided to pursue culinary as well as academic endeavours. A teaching role at Auckland Seafood School over the last eight years has seen him progress from kitchen assistant to teaching chef; Colin also works part-time in the Chemical and Materials Engineering Department at the University of Auckland. As a passionate cook and scientist, Colin has the ability to explain why things are done the way they are in a given recipe. Colin has a passion for many cuisines, with Mexican, Cajun, Italian and Japanese being among his favourites.

Mark Dronjak's cooking passions are flavour and presentation, along with a freestyle approach. A chef with over 30 years' experience in hospitality, one of Mark's career highlights was hosting a talkback radio show in Australia, 'Fine Food Down Under', often live from the kitchen. He is also a senior judge for New Zealand's chef competitions and has been published by numerous magazines – *Gourmet Traveller*, *Australian Fare* and *Condé Nast*, to name a few – and by various New Zealand and Australian newspapers. Mark lives on a lifestyle block in the Waitakere Ranges on Auckland's west coast, and is currently working on a cookbook. He is a passionate producer of artisan and handcrafted food products. **www.markdronjak.co.nz**

Marco Edwardes began his career at the Michelin-starred Laudensacks Parkhotel & Spa near his hometown in northern Bavaria/Germany. After completing his three-year apprenticeship, he worked in various other top restaurants around Germany, obtaining a master's diploma (Meisterbrief) in his craft. He moved to New Zealand in 1998 and became head chef at the renowned Pegasus Bay Winery in Waipara. Two years later he took his family to Switzerland, where Marco worked as head chef at an exclusive guesthouse. Returning to New Zealand in 2006, Marco was appointed head chef at award-winning Te Whau Vineyard and Restaurant on Waiheke Island. With a cooking style tending towards fresh, modern New Zealand cuisine with a classical European base, Marco likes to keep things simple and flavoursome.

A trained nutritionist, **Petra New** qualified as a chef in 1989 and worked her way around the world, soaking up the flavours of each country she spent time in. Career highlights include her time as the Mayor of Edinburgh's personal chef and as part of a catering team for the Queen's garden tea parties at Holyrood Palace. Petra has worked in Auckland restaurants Hammerheads, Iguaçu, Halo and One Tree Grill. Now the mother of two energetic boys, she owns a boutique catering company, creates amazing cakes and tutors at the Auckland Seafood School. Petra's food philosophy is all about creating modern, uncomplicated and innovative cuisine, using fresh, local and seasonal ingredients.

Steve Roberts is a multi-award-winning chef with an infectious passion for cooking. After classical professional training, Steve decided travel was on the cards. This led him to Australia and then on to Japan for six years, where he soaked up the nuances of Japanese cuisine. Returning to New Zealand, he has since led the kitchens at The Hunting Lodge, Hotel du Vin, Sileni Estate, the Spencer on Byron Hotel and Nosh Gourmet. His company Foodcreationz specialises in catering for private dinner parties, cocktail parties and boardroom catering as well as menu-design consultancy.
foodcreationz@xtra.co.nz

Glossary

al dente: Cooked through but still offering resistance to the bite.

Arborio rice: Italian rice variety with high starch content and a medium grain. Its creamy texture when cooked is excellent for risottos.

arrowroot: A starch used as a thickening agent in cooking.

balsamic reduction: Balsamic vinegar that has been reduced to a syrupy consistency. Can be used in both sweet and savoury dishes.

baste: Keep an item moist and full of flavour by periodically coating it with its own juices or extra sauce.

béchamel: Also known as white sauce. Made by adding milk to roux.

bouillon: A clear, seasoned broth made from boiling together meat, poultry or vegetables.

bouquet garni: A bundle of herbs tied together with culinary string, or placed into a sachet, boiled with other ingredients to impart its flavour and removed before the dish is served. A standard bouquet garni usually consists of sprigs of thyme and parsley and bay leaves.

cartouche: Baking paper (folded and then cut into a circle) used to cover cooked food.

chermoula: A North African spice paste containing a mixture of herbs, garlic, olive oil and seasoning.

chorizo: A Spanish-style cured sausage, spicy, smoky and deep red in colour.

dashi: A Japanese cooking stock used as a base in soups.

deglazing: Adding liquid to a warm pan after cooking seafood or meat, to remove baked-on pieces and further flavour the dish.

fish sauce: Made from the fermentation of fish and sea salt. A staple in many Asian cuisines.

flaky sea salt: Pure, uniform cubic crystal shapes formed when sea water is evaporated.

galangal: Also known in Thailand as ginza, galangal is a spice resembling ginger, but more peppery. It can be purchased in root form in some vegetable shops or frozen from Asian supermarkets.

gratin: To bake or grill to form a golden crust.

harissa: A fiery North African spice paste with chilli, coriander, cumin, garlic, caraway, salt and olive oil.

horopito: Peppery-tasting leaves of the New Zealand native shrub (*Pseudowintera colorata*), available from specialty shops.

julienne: To cut into long, thin strips.

Kaffir lime leaves: An essential ingredient in Thai cuisine. Tear rather than cut; if cut, leaves will leave their oils (flavour) behind on the knife.

karengo: Edible seaweed in dried form.

kawakawa: New Zealand pepper tree; both the seeds and the leaves have culinary uses.

kecap manis: A thick Indonesian soy sauce sweetened with palm sugar.

kombu: Edible seaweed (available fresh or dried). An essential ingredient in dashi, a Japanese soup stock.

lemongrass: Herb widely used in Asian cuisine and an essential ingredient in Thai dishes. The stalks release a lemony flavour when crushed/bruised.

masa harina: A traditional Mexican flour, made from corn, used to make tortillas.

micro greens: Baby leaves used as a salad blend. Available from supermarkets and specialty food stores.

mirin: Japanese rice wine with a mild, sweet flavour and a lower alcohol content than sake. It is a key ingredient in teriyaki sauce.

nage: A flavoursome French stock made from vegetables, fish and herbs.

New York cut pepper: Pepper that is granulated, not ground. Available from specialty food stores. An alternative is freshly ground black pepper.

non-reactive (bowls, pans): A non-reactive bowl (glass, plastic or stainless steel) or saucepan (stainless steel) won't react chemically when using acidic ingredients.

palm sugar: The sap of certain palm trees, boiled until thick. Creates a solid, sweet syrupy block that can be used in cooking and dressings.

panko: Japanese breadcrumb variety used as a light and crunchy coating for fried foods. Available from Asian supermarkets.

paprika: Spice available in several varieties: Spanish smoked, Spanish sweet and Hungarian (which is more bitter and darker than the Spanish varieties).

Parmesan and Parmigiano Reggiano: Hard, dry, sharply flavoured cheese. Parmigiano is usually better quality.

purée: Blend to create a creamy paste.

quenelle: A shape formed by passing ingredients such as ice cream, pastes, crème fraîche and so on between two spoons to create an oval-like form.

refresh: To immerse cooked food in cold water to cool it quickly and stop the cooking process.

rest (fish): Leave in a warm spot for 1–2 minutes to redistribute proteins back into the fish.

rice wine: Beverage made from fermenting rice starch. Used extensively in Asian cooking.

roulade: To roll. Can apply to both sweet and savoury dishes.

roux: A classical French combination of butter and flour cooked on the stovetop and used to thicken sauces.

semi-dried and sun-dried tomatoes: Tomatoes dried slowly at a low temperature to produce a concentrated flavour. Stored in a jar with olive oil, they have an extended shelf life.

shrimp paste: Fermented ground shrimp mixed with salt. It has a very strong flavour and is used a lot in Asian cooking.

somen noodles: A very thin Japanese noodle made from wheat flour, available at any supermarket or Asian grocery store.

tamarind: Pod-like fruit produced by a leguminous tree, which has a sweet/sour flavour. Tamarind can be purchased as a paste/pulp or as tamarind water/juice, and is used in various cuisines around the world.

verjuice: The acidic juice of crab apples, unripe grapes or other sour fruit.

vincotto: Slow-cooked unfermented grape must reduced to create a dark, sweet full-flavoured syrup.

wonton wrappers: Flour, egg, water and salt made into a pastry then cut to shape.

Index

Italicised numbers refer to a species' entry in the visual identification guide on pages 20–29.

A

aioli 162, 189, 257; *see also* mayonnaise
    Barbecue-seared five-spice squid with wasabi aioli 134
    Bouillabaisse 257
    mustard & tarragon aioli 224
    Salt & pepper squid with sweet chilli & wasabi aioli 171
    Scampi with kawakawa aioli 53
    splitting 189
    sun-dried tomato aioli 189
alfonsino *21*
    Crispy alfonsino, chorizo & chickpea salad 98
    Crispy-skinned alfonsino with creamy sweetcorn & crab risotto 124
almond couscous, Moroccan fish with 180
anchovies
    anchovy dressing 82
    black olive tapenade 194
    Caesar dressing 263
    green salsa 268
    olive butter 270
    Poppy seed & tuna triangles 32
    salsa verde 73
    sauce remoulade 264
apple: Chargrilled maple & apple salmon steaks 148
Asian crab cakes with peanut & sweet chilli dipping sauce 42
Asian herb & chilli linguine with marinated salmon skewers 123
Asian spices: Barbecued chilli squid with Asian spices & green beans 140
asparagus 143, 253
avocado
    avocado salsa 149
    Mexican-style prawn cocktail 62
    Open prawn wontons 98
    Sushi & sashimi 78

B

Baby Mediterranean fishcakes with tzatziki 100
bacon *see also* pancetta
    Bacon-wrapped salmon on portobello mushrooms 189
    Italian-style cockles 58
    Mussel chowder 254
    Oysters Kilpatrick 48
    Paella 110
    Pipi soup, bach-style 249
    Seafood chowder 254
    Ultimate seafood mixed grill 158
Baked fish with Mediterranean crumble 234
Baked market fish with white bean purée, fennel salad & orange oil 231

Baked white fish with Pernod cream sauce & potatoes 236
baked whole fish/fish fillets 17
    Trevally baked in a citrus salt crust 224
Balinese fried fish 186
balsamic mushrooms 138
bamboo shoots
    Fish head soup 244
    Prawn & squid noodle box 114
banana leaves: Kingfish baked in banana leaves 212
barbecue fish fillets 16
Barbecue-seared five-spice squid with wasabi aioli 134
Barbecued black bean salmon fillet on ginger & sesame vegetables 137
Barbecued chilli squid with Asian spices & green beans 140
Barbecued corn & prawn fritters 50
Barbecued fish with hot & sour chilli sauce 138
Barbecued bluenose on crushed potatoes with caper, lemon & olive dressing 155
Barbecued seafood platter with charred vegetables & rosemary potatoes 132
Barbecued sticky Chinese orange & ginger snapper parcels 154
Barbecued tandoori prawn & pineapple skewers with minted yoghurt 79
barracouta *21*
basil
    dried tomato & basil butter 270
    tomato & basil dressing 112, 178
    tomato & basil salsa 268
    Whole snapper steamed with ginger, basil & chilli 222
batter
    beer batter 186
    flour & egg battered fish 261
    tempura batter 176
    yeast batter 260
bean sprouts 102, 119, 126
beans: black beans, butterbeans, fava beans, white beans; *see also* cannellini beans; green beans
    Baked market fish with white bean purée 231
    Barbecued black bean salmon fillet on ginger & sesame vegetables 137
    Market fish with butterbean purée, scallops & chorizo with salsa verde 196
    Pan-seared John Dory with creamy roasted capsicums & refried beans 182
    Seafood & chorizo with fava beans 216
    Wok-fried black bean pipi 86
beer
    Beer-battered fish fillets 186
    Smoked salmon, leek & beer fritters with garlic mayonnaise 101
beetroot & feta salad 72
Bengali-style fish curry 232
beurre blanc 160

Hot-smoked salmon with potato cakes & beurre blanc 160
    lemon beurre blanc 70
bisque, crayfish 256
Black pepper market fish salad 67
Bloody Mary mixture, with kina 50
blue cod *21*, 49
    Pan-fried cod on risotto 115
    Smoked fish mousse 49
blue moki *21*
blue whiting, southern *21*
bluenose *21*
    Barbecued bluenose on crushed potatoes with caper, lemon & olive dressing 155
    Market fish with butterbean purée, scallops & chorizo 196
boar fish: Gratin of white fish, scallops & prawns with karengo 210
bok choy
    Grilled fish fillets with bok choy & mandarin & ginger sauce 136
    Tea-steamed salmon 238
Bouillabaisse 257
bread *see* bruschetta; ciabatta; crostini
breadcrumbs, panko breadcrumbs
    Baked fish with Mediterranean crumble 234
    Crumbed fish 261
    Grilled prawns with tomato, feta & dill 150
    Herb & panko crumbed fish fillets 166
    Mussels grilled with peppercorns 54
    Panko mussels filled with chorizo & mozzarella 46
brill *21*, 70
broadbill
    marinated skewers 123
    Fennel-crusted, with olive oil-crushed potatoes 178
    Hot-smoked broadbill with mash & caper sauce 215
    Pan-fried broadbill in a saffron sauce 200
broccoli 210
broth *see* soup
bruschetta
    Bruschetta with seared octopus 156
    Bruschetta with tuna tartare 35
burgers: Fish burgers 162
butterbean purée 196
butterfish *22*
butters, flavoured 270

C

cabbage 126
Cajun spice mix 146, 156, 160, 215, 219, 261
cakes *see* crab cakes; fishcakes; fritters
cannellini beans 58, 172
capers 168
    black olive tapenade 194
    caper, lemon & olive dressing 155
    caper & olive dressing 220
    caper sauce 215
    green salsa 268

Hot-smoked broadbill with mash &
    caper sauce 215
Salmon with caper & olive
    dressing 220
salsa verde 196
sauce tartare 266
capsicum
    avocado salsa 149
    Barbecued snapper parcels 154
    Charred vegetables 132
    chilli sauce 267
    Crispy-skinned snapper with red
        capsicum & fennel confit & black
        olive tapenade 194
    Fish & tomato Spanish-style stew 214
    Ginger & sesame vegetables 137
    Kasbah mussels with tomatoes,
        coriander, olives & capsicum 159
    Mixed seafood & vegetable stir-fry 188
    Paella 110
    Pan-seared John Dory with creamy
        roasted capsicums & refried
        beans 182
    paprika & red pepper mayonnaise 265
    Poached monkfish in potato & tomato
        casserole 228
    red capsicum & fennel confit 194
    Sea cucumber with sorbet 88
    Seafood gumbo 219
    Sushi & sashimi 78
    tomato & basil dressing 178
cardinal fish, black *22*
carrot
    Barbecued snapper parcels 154
    carrot fritters 209
    Charred vegetables 132
    Eggplant-topped fish fillets with carrot
        fritters & dill yoghurt 209
    Ginger & sesame vegetables 137
    Mixed seafood & vegetable stir-fry 188
    Summer vegetables 253
    Thai vegetable rice noodles 126
    Vietnamese prawn rice paper wraps 66
cashews
    Mixed seafood & vegetable stir-fry with
        cashew nuts 188
    Prawn & papaya salad 102
    Prawn & squid noodle box 114
cauliflower: Snapper on curry-spiced
    cauliflower florets with coconut cream
    & lychee foam 198
ceviche
    Fish ceviche 45
    Salmon ceviche with fresh tortilla
        chips 34
Chargrilled fish fillets with balsamic
    mushrooms 138
Chargrilled maple & apple salmon steaks,
    baked potatoes & fennel slaw 148
cheese *see also specific cheeses*, e.g. feta;
    goat's cheese; Parmesan
    Fish tartlets with fresh herbs 204
    Panko mussels filled with chorizo &
        mozzarella 46
    Seafood crêpes 97
    Two-cheese tortellini with seared scallops
        & tomato & basil dressing 112
Chenin Blanc nage with a seafood medley
    & summer vegetables 253
chermoula, chermoula dressing 206, 261

cherry tomato 86, 143, 171, 184, 196, 242;
    see also tomato
chèvre *see* goat's cheese
chicken
    Jambalaya 214
    Paella 110
chickpeas: Crispy alfonsino, chorizo &
    chickpea salad 98
chilli
    Asian herb & chilli linguine with
        marinated salmon skewers 123
    Barbecued chilli squid with Asian spices
        & green beans 140
    chilli jam 143
    chilli sauce 267
    Coconut & chilli seafood parcels 92
    Crispy tiger prawns with lime &
        chilli 144
    hot & sour chilli sauce 138
    hot & sour dressing 104
    Mexican-style prawn cocktail 62
    nuoc cham dipping sauce 266
    peanut & sweet chilli dipping sauce 42
    Prawn & squid noodle box 114
    removing seeds 119
    Salt & pepper squid with sweet chilli &
        wasabi aioli 171
    Spicy scallop & noodle soup 250
    sweet chilli & wasabi aioli 171
    Thai hot & sour prawn soup 245
    Thai red curry paste 271
    White fish with chilli, Mexican herbs &
        green olives 89
    Whole snapper steamed with ginger,
        basil & chilli 222
Chinese five-spice
    Barbecue-seared five-spice squid 134
    Barbecued sticky Chinese orange &
        ginger snapper parcels 154
chips
    tortilla chips 34, 62
chorizo
    Crispy alfonsino, chorizo & chickpea
        salad 98
    Market fish with butterbean purée, scallops
        & chorizo with salsa verde 196
    Paella 110
    Panko mussels filled with chorizo &
        mozzarella 46
    Prawn & chorizo skewers with beetroot
        & feta salad 72
    Seafood & chorizo with fava beans 216
    Snapper & chorizo tacos 64
    Ultimate seafood mixed grill 158
chowder *see also* soup
    Mussel chowder 254
    Seafood chowder 254
choy sum 137
ciabatta *see also* bruschetta
    Fish burgers 162
    Mussels grilled with peppercorns 54
    Ultimate seafood mixed grill 158
citrus *see also* lemon, lime
    citrus & black pepper dressing 168
    citrus mayonnaise 158
    citrus & palm sugar dressing 263
    Citrus paua with herbed butter 38
    Gravadlax 54
    grilled citrus 271

Tortellini of prawns, fish & mushrooms
    in seafood citrus broth 129
Trevally baked in a citrus salt crust 224
clams *see* cockles
cockles/clams *22*, 58
    Chenin Blanc nage with a seafood
        medley & summer vegetables 253
    Clams with spaghetti, saffron & leek 126
    Fettuccine with seasonal seafood, rocket
        & lemon 122
    Italian-style cockles 58
    Seafood & chorizo with fava beans 216
    Tuatua soup 252
coconut, coconut cream
    Coconut & chilli seafood parcels 92
    Fish ceviche 45
    in curry 216, 225, 234, 238
    Mussel, coconut & tamarind salad 104
    Pumpkin soup 247
    Sea cucumber with sorbet 88
    Snapper on curry-spiced cauliflower
        florets with coconut cream & lychee
        foam 198
    Thai red curry & coconut cream
        emulsion 238
cod *see* blue cod
consommé: Fish consommé 248
cooking methods 15–17
    bake whole fish 17
    barbecue 16
    pan-fry 15
    poach 17
    steam whole fish 16
corn, baby corn
    Barbecued corn & prawn fritters 50
    Crispy-skinned alfonsino with creamy
        sweetcorn & crab risotto 124
    Prawn, fish & corn steamed
        moneybags 36
    Prawn & squid noodle box 114
corn (masa harina)
    corn tortillas 272; *see also* tortillas
    tortilla chips 34, 62
courgette
    Barbecued snapper parcels 154
    Charred vegetables 132
    Ginger & sesame vegetables 137
    Mixed seafood & vegetable stir-fry 188
    Mussel fritters 80
    risotto 116
    Scallop & goat's cheese fritters 67
    Warm squid salad 76
court bouillon (for poaching) 17
couscous 206
    Moroccan fish with almond couscous 180
crab, crabmeat
    Asian crab cakes with peanut & sweet
        chilli dipping sauce 42
    Barbecued corn & prawn fritters 50
    Crispy-skinned alfonsino with creamy
        sweetcorn & crab risotto 124
    Paddle crabs 94
    Seafood gumbo 219
    Sweet & sour wok-fried crab 193
crayfish/rock lobster *22*, 246
    Crayfish bisque with leek & prawns 256
    Grilled crayfish 152
    Japanese crayfish soup 246
    Wok-fried, with lemongrass &
        tamarind 170

cream
    beurre blanc 160
    Fettuccine with seasonal seafood, rocket
        & lemon 122
    Gratin of white fish, scallops & prawns
        with karengo 210
    herb & mustard cream sauce 218
    Mussel chowder 254
    Mussels grilled with peppercorns 54
    Pernod cream sauce 236
    Poached seafood roulade, spinach &
        sauce vierge 68
cream cheese
    Open prawn wontons 98
    Smoked kahawai pâté 48
crème fraîche 54, 115, 253, 254
    lime crème fraîche 64
crêpes, seafood 97
Crispy alfonsino, chorizo & chickpea
    salad 98
Crispy tiger prawns with lime & chilli 144
Crispy-skinned alfonsino with creamy
    sweetcorn & crab risotto 124
Crispy-skinned snapper with mushrooms,
    ginger & tropical fruit salsa 183
Crispy-skinned snapper with red capsicum
    & fennel confit & black olive
    tapenade 194
crostini, garlic 242
croutons 76
Crumbed fish 261
cucumber 42, 119
    in ceviche 34, 45
    Sushi & sashimi 78
    Teriyaki salmon with somen noodle
        salad 120
    tzatziki 100
    Vietnamese prawn rice paper wraps 66
curry *see also* Thai red curry
    Bengali-style fish curry 232
    curry paste 225, 232
    Kedgeree 118
    Mussels steamed in Thai red curry with
        citrus 234
    Scallop & potato Panang curry 225
    Snapper on curry-spiced cauliflower
        florets with coconut cream & lychee
        foam 198
    Tea-steamed salmon with Thai red curry
        & coconut cream emulsion 238
    Thai red curry with fish 216

D

dashi: Japanese crayfish soup 246
dates 180
dill
    dill butter 270
    dill dressing 262
    dill yoghurt 209
    Grilled prawns with tomato, feta &
        dill 150
dipping sauce *see also* mayonnaise; sauce
    minted yoghurt dipping sauce 79
    Nuoc cham dipping sauce 266
    peanut & sweet chilli dipping sauce 42
    Teppanyaki dipping sauce 266
    Vietnamese dipping sauce 66
dressing *see also* mayonnaise
    anchovy dressing 82

basic vinaigrette 262
Caesar dressing 263
caper, lemon & olive dressing 155
caper & olive dressing 220
chermoula dressing 206
citrus & black pepper dressing 168
citrus & palm sugar dressing 263
dill dressing 262
eggplant dip 85
green olive dressing 58
honey & ginger vinaigrette 262
hot & sour dressing 104
lemongrass dressing 102
ponzu vinaigrette 86
spicy yoghurt & harissa dressing 263
spinach yoghurt dressing 263
tomato & basil dressing 112, 178
tzatziki 100
vinaigrette 88, 262
warm tomato vinaigrette 262
dukkah 132, 260

E

eel, long-finned eel *22*, 52
    Smoked eel with mustard mousse 52
egg
    Barbecued corn & prawn fritters 50
    Eggs Benedict with salmon on kumara
        cakes & orange Hollandaise 199
    Fish tartlets with fresh herbs 204
    fresh egg pasta dough 272
    Japanese crayfish soup 246
    Kedgeree 118
    Nasi goreng 119
    Seared tuna Niçoise 174
    Ultimate seafood mixed grill 158
    Whitebait flan 74
    Whitebait fritters 80
egg pasta dough, fresh 272
    Open ravioli with snapper 115
    Two-cheese tortellini with seared
        scallops 112
eggplant
    Charred vegetables 132
    eggplant dip 85
    eggplant relish 143
    Eggplant-topped fish fillets with carrot
        fritters & dill yoghurt 209
    Fishcakes topped with eggplant dip 85
    Grilled fish fillets with chilli jam-spiced
        eggplant relish & green beans 143
    Market fish with eggplant, tomato &
        mozzarella 228
    spiced eggplant relish 143
    Thai red curry with fish 216

F

fennel 168, 184, 237
    Bouillabaisse 257
    Fennel-crusted kingfish with olive oil-
        crushed potatoes 178
    fennel salad 231
    fennel slaw 148
    fennel spice mix 90, 178
    red capsicum & fennel confit 194
    Salad of fennel-crusted kingfish with
        orange, watercress, fennel & olives 90
    Baked market fish with white bean purée,

    fennel salad & orange oil 231
feta
    Grilled prawns with tomato, feta &
        dill 150
    Mediterranean-inspired whole baked
        fish 208
    Monkfish, tomato & feta tarts 62
    Prawn & chorizo skewers with beetroot
        & feta salad 72
Fettuccine with seasonal seafood, rocket &
    lemon 122
filo pastry: Poppy seed & tuna triangles 32
fish *see also specific fish*; raw fish; salmon;
    smoked fish
    Baby Mediterranean fishcakes with
        tzatziki 100
    Baked fish with Mediterranean
        crumble 234
    Baked market fish with white bean
        purée, fennel salad & orange oil 231
    Baked white fish with Pernod cream
        sauce & potatoes 236
    Balinese fried fish 186
    Barbecued fish with hot & sour chilli
        sauce 138
    battered fish 186, 261
    Beer-battered fish fillets 186
    Bengali-style fish curry 232
    Black pepper market fish salad 67
    boning & skinning fish 14
    Chargrilled fish fillets with balsamic
        mushrooms 138
    Coconut & chilli seafood parcels 92
    Crispy-skinned alfonsino with creamy
        sweetcorn & crab risotto 124
    crumbed fish 261
    Eggplant-topped fish fillets with carrot
        fritters & dill yoghurt 209
    Fettuccine with seasonal seafood, rocket
        & lemon 122
    filleting fish 14, 15
    fish balls 245
    Fish burgers 162
    Fish ceviche 45
    Fish consommé 248
    Fish head soup 244
    Fish pie with puff pastry 237
    fish stock *see separate entry*
    Fish tartlets with fresh herbs 204
    Fish, tomato & lemongrass soup 250
    Fish & tomato Spanish-style stew 214
    Fish velouté 49, 249
    Fishcakes topped with eggplant dip 85
    Flour & egg battered fish 261
    Garlic & ginger sautéed fish with
        pumpkin soup 247
    Ginger & manuka-honey glazed hot-
        smoked kahawai with avocado
        salsa 149
    Gratin of white fish, scallops & prawns
        with karengo 210
    Grilled fish fillets with bok choy &
        mandarin & ginger sauce 136
    Grilled fish fillets with chilli jam-spiced
        eggplant relish & green beans 143
    gutting fish 12
    Herb & panko crumbed fish fillets 166
    Herb-crusted fish fillets with bean &
        potato salad & salsa verde 73

Market fish with butterbean purée, scallops & chorizo with salsa verde 196
Market fish with eggplant, tomato & mozzarella 228
Mediterranean-inspired whole baked fish 208
Mixed seafood & vegetable stir-fry with cashew nuts 188
Moroccan-baked chermoula fish with couscous 206
Moroccan fish ball soup 245
Moroccan fish with almond couscous 180
Paella 110
Poached seafood roulade, spinach & sauce vierge 68
Prawn, fish & corn steamed moneybags 36
Red wine risotto with sautéed squid & seasonal white fish 116
scaling fish 12
Seafood chowder 254
Seafood citrus broth 129
Seafood soup with garlic crostini 242
smoked *see* smoked fish
Snapper with green pea purée & crispy shrimp polenta 184
stock *see* fish stock
Sushi & sashimi 78
Thai red curry with fish 216
Tortellini of prawns, fish & mushrooms in seafood citrus broth 129
White fish with chilli, Mexican herbs & green olives 89
Whole barbecue-grilled market fish with Greek potato mash 146
Fish head soup 244
fish stock 272; *see also* soup
beurre blanc 160
Fish consommé 248
Fish velouté 249
Seafood citrus broth 129
Seafood soup 242
fishcakes
Baby Mediterranean fishcakes with tzatziki 100
Fishcakes topped with eggplant dip 85
five spice *see* Chinese five spice
flounder, yellowbelly flounder *22, 23*, 174
Flounder paupiettes with prawns, spinach & lemon beurre blanc 70
Grilled flounder 156
Whole pan-seared flounder 174
fritters *see also* fishcakes
Barbecued corn & prawn fritters 50
Carrot fritters 209
Mussel fritters 80
Scallop & goat's cheese fritters 67
Smoked salmon, leek & beer fritters with garlic mayonnaise 101
Whitebait fritters 80
frostfish *23*

G
garlic *see also* aioli
Caesar dressing 263
Charred vegetables 132
garlic crostini 242
Garlic & ginger sautéed fish with

pumpkin soup 247
garlic & herb butter 270
garlic mayonnaise 45, 101, 265
green salsa 268
garfish/piper *23*
gemfish *23*, 247
Garlic & ginger sautéed fish with pumpkin soup 247
ginger
Barbecued sticky Chinese orange & ginger snapper parcels 154
Crispy-skinned snapper with mushrooms, ginger & tropical fruit salsa 183
Garlic & ginger sautéed fish with pumpkin soup 247
Ginger & manuka-honey glazed hot-smoked kahawai with avocado salsa 149
Ginger & sesame vegetables 137
Grilled fish fillets with bok choy & mandarin & ginger sauce 136
honey & ginger vinaigrette 262
Prawn & squid noodle box 114
Whole snapper steamed with ginger, basil & chilli 222
glaze
lime glaze 74, 264
orange & Pernod glaze 264
goat's cheese, chèvre
Scallop & goat's cheese fritters 67
Two-cheese tortellini with seared scallops & tomato & basil dressing 112
Gravadlax 54
Gratin of white fish, scallops & prawns with karengo 210
Greek potato mash 146
green beans
Barbecued chilli squid with Asian spices & green beans 140
Grilled fish fillets with chilli jam-spiced eggplant relish & green beans 143
Herb-crusted fish fillets with bean & potato salad & salsa verde 73
Seared snapper on potato & green bean salad with watercress pesto 177
Seared tuna Niçoise 174
geoduck 193
green pea purée 184
green salsa 268
grey mullet *23*
Grilled Caesar salad with barbecued scallops & prawns 82
Grilled crayfish (rock lobster) 152
Grilled fish fillets with bok choy & mandarin & ginger sauce 136
Grilled fish fillets with chilli jam-spiced eggplant relish & green beans 143
Grilled flounder 156
Grilled kingfish skewers with lime & lemongrass sauce 61
grilled citrus 271; *see also* lemon; lime
Grilled prawns with tomato, feta & dill 150
Gruyère: Fish tartlets with fresh herbs 204
gumbo: Seafood gumbo 219
gurnard 210; *see also* fish
Baby Mediterranean fishcakes with tzatziki 100
Beer-battered fish fillets 186

Fish burgers 162
Fishcakes topped with eggplant dip 85
Gratin of white fish, scallops & prawns with karengo 210
Paella 110
Seafood soup with garlic crostini 242
Seared fillets, with semi-dried tomatoes & fresh herbs 172
Tortellini of prawns, fish & mushrooms in seafood citrus broth 129

H
hake *23*
ham: Jambalaya 214
hapuku *23*; *see also* fish
Baked white fish with Pernod cream sauce & potatoes 236
Barbecued fish with hot & sour chilli sauce 138
Bengali-style fish curry 232
Chenin Blanc nage with a seafood medley & summer vegetables 253
Fish, tomato & lemongrass soup 250
Fish & tomato Spanish-style stew 214
Gratin of white fish, scallops & prawns with karengo 210
Herb-crusted fish fillets with bean & potato salad & salsa verde 73
Market fish with butterbean purée, scallops & chorizo with salsa verde 196
Mixed seafood & vegetable stir-fry with cashew nuts 188
Pan-fried hapuku with sautéed potatoes 190
Poached, in potato & tomato casserole 228
Red wine risotto with sautéed squid & seasonal white fish 116
Smoked fish & spinach pies 220
Tea-steamed, with Thai red curry & coconut cream emulsion 238
Thai red curry with fish 216
White fish with chilli, Mexican herbs & green olives 89
harissa: spicy yoghurt & harissa dressing 263
Herb & panko crumbed fish fillets 166
Herb-crusted fish fillets with bean & potato salad & salsa verde 73
hoki *23*, 162
Beer-battered fish fillets 186
Fish burgers 162
Hollandaise 199, 220, 265
orange Hollandaise 199
honey
Ginger & manuka-honey glazed hot-smoked kahawai with avocado salsa 149
honey & ginger vinaigrette 262
horopito: Mussel chowder 254
hot & sour chilli sauce 138
hot & sour dressing 104
hot-smoked *see also* smoked fish
Hot-smoked broadbill with mash & caper sauce 215
Hot-smoked salmon with potato cakes & beurre blanc 160

I

Italian-style cockles 58

J

jack mackerel *24*
Jambalaya 214
Japanese crayfish soup 246
John Dory *24*, 136; *see also* fish
    Grilled fish fillets with bok choy &
        mandarin & ginger sauce 136
    Pan-seared John Dory with creamy roasted
        capsicums & refried beans 182

K

Kaffir lime leaf 104, 144, 170, 216, 225,
    234, 244, 245, 247, 250, 271
kahawai *24*, 48; *see also* fish
    Ginger & manuka-honey glazed hot-
        smoked kahawai with avocado
        salsa 149
    Mixed seafood & vegetable stir-fry with
        cashew nuts 188
    Smoked kahawai pâté 48
    Smoked fish puffs with garlic
        mayonnaise 45
karengo seaweed: Gratin of white fish,
    scallops & prawns with karengo 210
Kasbah mussels with tomatoes, coriander,
    olives & capsicum 159
katsuobushi (bonito flakes) *see* dashi
kawakawa 210, 276
    kawakawa aioli 53
Kedgeree 118
kina/sea urchin/sea egg, kina roe *24*, 50
    Kina Bloody Mary 50
king prawn *see also* prawn
    Prosciutto-wrapped prawn skewers 58
kingfish, yellowtail *24*, 138
    Asian herb & chilli linguine with
        marinated salmon/kingfish
        skewers 123
    Barbecued fish with hot & sour chilli
        sauce 138
    Chargrilled fish fillets with balsamic
        mushrooms 138
    Chenin Blanc nage with a seafood
        medley & summer vegetables 253
    Fennel-crusted kingfish with olive oil-
        crushed potatoes 178
    Grilled kingfish skewers with lime &
        lemongrass sauce 61
    Kingfish with a Mexican spice paste
        baked in banana leaves 212
    Mixed seafood & vegetable stir-fry with
        cashew nuts 188
    Salad of fennel-crusted kingfish with
        orange, watercress, fennel &
        olives 90
    Tea-steamed, with Thai red curry &
        coconut cream emulsion 238
    Teriyaki, with somen noodle salad 120
    Thai red curry with fish 216
kombu *see* dashi
kumara
    Eggs Benedict with salmon on kumara
        cakes & orange Hollandaise 199
    Mussel chowder 254

L

leatherjacket/creamfish *24*, 234
    Thai red curry with fish 216
leek 61, 244
    Clams with spaghetti, saffron & leek 126
    Crayfish bisque with leek & prawns 256
    Fish pie 237
    Leek & oyster spoons 44
    Seafood citrus broth 129
    Seafood soup with garlic crostini 242
    Seared scallops with vanilla leek &
        pineapple & melon salsa 106
    Smoked salmon, leek & beer fritters
        with garlic mayonnaise 101
    Tuatua soup 252
lemon *see also* citrus; preserved lemon
    caper, lemon & olive dressing 155
    Fettuccine with seasonal seafood, rocket
        & lemon 122
    grilled lemon halves 132, 146, 152, 156,
        166, 174, 186, 206
    lemon beurre blanc 70
    lemon mayonnaise 40
lemon sole *24*
lemonfish/rig *24*
    Barbecued, on crushed potatoes with
        caper, lemon & olive dressing 155
    Herb-crusted fish fillets with bean &
        potato salad & salsa verde 73
lemongrass
    Fish head soup 244
    Fish, tomato & lemongrass soup 250
    Grilled kingfish skewers with lime &
        lemongrass sauce 61
    Prawn & papaya salad with lemongrass
        dressing 102
    Wok-fried prawns with lemongrass &
        tamarind 170
lettuce 236; *see also* micro greens
    Grilled Caesar salad with barbecued
        scallops & prawns 82
    Minted lettuce scampi cups 53
    Prawn & papaya salad 102
    Vietnamese prawn rice paper wraps 66
lime *see also* citrus
    coconut cream emulsion 238
    Crispy tiger prawns with lime &
        chilli 144
    Grilled kingfish skewers with lime &
        lemongrass sauce 61
    grilled lime halves 132, 144, 182
    hot & sour chilli sauce 138
    lime crème fraîche 64
    lime glaze 74, 264
    lime & peppercorn butter 270
    nuoc cham dipping sauce 266
ling 25, 253; *see also* fish
    Barbecued, on crushed potatoes with
        caper, lemon & olive dressing 155
    Bengali-style fish curry 232
    Chenin Blanc nage with a seafood
        medley & summer vegetables 253
    Ling on curry-spiced cauliflower florets
        with coconut cream & lychee
        foam 198
    White fish with chilli, Mexican herbs &
        green olives 89
linguine *see* pasta

lychee foam: Snapper on curry-spiced
    cauliflower florets with coconut
    cream & lychee foam 198

M

macadamia & rocket pesto 269
mandarin & ginger sauce 136
mango, caramelised 44
manuka honey & ginger glazed hot-
    smoked kahawai 149
manuka smoke mix 149
Maori potato gratin 210
maple syrup: Chargrilled maple & apple
    salmon steaks 148
marinade, seafood 264; *see also* spices
marinara mix
    Seafood chowder 254
    Seafood crêpes 97
Marinated salmon skewers 123
Market fish with butterbean purée, scallops
    & chorizo with salsa verde 196
Market fish with eggplant, tomato &
    mozzarella 228
mayonnaise 265, 266
    citrus mayonnaise 158
    garlic mayonnaise 45, 101, 265
    lemon mayonnaise 40
    paprika & red pepper mayonnaise 265
Mediterranean-inspired whole baked
    fish 208
Mediterranean-style grilled scampi 144
melon, rock melon
    Seared scallops with vanilla leek &
        pineapple & melon salsa 106
    tropical fruit salsa 183
mesclun 67, 144
Mexican spice paste 212
Mexican-style prawn cocktail 62
micro greens 64, 86
Minted lettuce scampi cups 53
Mixed seafood & vegetable stir-fry with
    cashew nuts 188
monkfish/stargazer 25, 172; *see also* fish
    Asian herb & chilli linguine with
        marinated fish skewers 123
    Bengali-style fish curry 232
    Bouillabaisse 257
    Chenin Blanc nage with a seafood
        medley & summer vegetables 253
    Fish tartlets with fresh herbs 204
    Herb-crusted fish fillets with bean &
        potato salad & salsa verde 73
    Monkfish, tomato & feta tarts 62
    Poached monkfish in potato & tomato
        casserole 228
    Red wine risotto with sautéed squid &
        seasonal white fish 116
    Tea-steamed, with Thai red curry &
        coconut cream emulsion 238
    Thai red curry with fish 216
    White fish with chilli, Mexican herbs &
        green olives 89
moonfish 25
Moroccan-baked chermoula fish with
    couscous 206
Moroccan fish ball soup 245
Moroccan fish with almond couscous 180
Moroccan spice mix 158, 180

mousse
    Smoked eel with mustard mousse 52
    Smoked fish mousse 49
mozzarella: Market fish with eggplant, tomato & mozzarella 228
mullet, smoked mullet
    baked in a citrus salt crust 224
    Bouillabaisse 257
    Smoked fish puffs with garlic mayonnaise 45
mushrooms, button/field/portobello; *see also* oyster mushrooms; shiitake mushrooms
    Bacon-wrapped salmon on portobello mushrooms 189
    Chargrilled fish fillets with balsamic mushrooms 138
    Mixed seafood & vegetable stir-fry 188
    Prawn & squid noodle box 114
    Salmon & spinach filo pie 218
    Spicy scallop & noodle soup 250
    Thai hot & sour prawn soup 245
    Ultimate seafood mixed grill 158
mussels *25*, 104
    Bouillabaisse 257
    Chenin Blanc nage with a seafood medley 253
    cleaning mussels 15
    Coconut & chilli seafood parcels 92
    Kasbah mussels with tomatoes, coriander, olives & capsicum 159
    Mussel chowder 254
    Mussel, coconut & tamarind salad 104
    Mussel fritters 80
    Mussels grilled with peppercorns 54
    Mussels steamed in Thai red curry with citrus 234
    Orange & sage barbecued mussels 150
    Panko mussels filled with chorizo & mozzarella 46
    Seafood & chorizo with fava beans 216
    Seafood chowder 254
    Seafood soup with garlic crostini 242
    Tuatua soup 252
mustard
    mustard mousse, with smoked eel 52
    mustard & tarragon aioli 224

N

nage: Chenin Blanc nage with a seafood medley & summer vegetables 253
Nasi goreng 119
New York cut pepper *see* pepper
noodles: bird nest/rice/somen
    Prawn & squid noodle box 114
    Spicy scallop & noodle soup 250
    Teriyaki salmon with somen noodle salad 120
    Thai vegetable rice noodles 126
nori *see* seaweed
nuoc cham dipping sauce 266

O

octopus
    Bouillabaisse 257
    Bruschetta with seared octopus 156
olives 228, 234
    black olive tapenade 194

caper, lemon & olive dressing 155
green olive dressing 58
green salsa 268
Kasbah mussels with tomatoes, coriander, olives & capsicum 159
Mediterranean-inspired whole baked fish 208
olive butter 270
olive oil-crushed potatoes 178
olive salsa 268
Parmesan & olive wafer stack with seared tuna 40
Salad of fennel-crusted kingfish with orange, watercress, fennel & olives 90
Salmon with caper & olive dressing 220
Seared tuna Niçoise 174
White fish with chilli, Mexican herbs & green olives 89
Open prawn wontons 98
Open ravioli with snapper 115
orange 98, 136
    Baked market fish with white bean purée, fennel salad & orange oil 231
    Barbecued sticky Chinese orange & ginger snapper parcels 154
    Kingfish with a Mexican spice paste baked in banana leaves 212
    orange Hollandaise 199
    orange oil 231
    orange Pernod glaze 264
    Orange & sage barbecued mussels 150
    Salad of fennel-crusted kingfish with orange, watercress, fennel & olives 90
    Eggs Benedict with salmon on kumara cakes & orange Hollandaise 199
orange roughy *27*, 49, 209
oreo, black/smooth/spiky *25*
oyster mushrooms: Oysters & salmon in Asian broth 244
oysters *25*, 39, 44
    Bluff oysters *25*, 44
    Leek & oyster spoons 44
    Oysters Kilpatrick 48
    Oysters Rockefeller 39
    Oysters & salmon in Asian broth 244
    Pacific oysters 39
    Seafood gumbo 219
    shucking oysters 15

P

paddle crabs *25*, 94
parore *25*
Paella 110
pancetta: refried beans 182
pan-fried fish 15–16
Pan-fried broadbill in a saffron sauce 200
Pan-fried cod on risotto 115
Pan-fried hapuku with sautéed potatoes 190
panko breadcrumbs *see* breadcrumbs
Pan-seared John Dory with creamy roasted capsicums & refried beans 182
papaya: Prawn & papaya salad with lemongrass dressing 102
Parmesan 35, 39, 210
    Parmesan & olive wafer stack with seared tuna 40
parsley
    green salsa 268
    salsa verde 73

parsnip: Fish pie with puff pastry 237
pasta *see also* noodles
    Asian herb & chilli linguine with marinated salmon skewers 123
    Clams with spaghetti, saffron & leek 126
    Fettuccine with seasonal seafood, rocket & lemon 122
    fresh egg pasta dough 272
    Open ravioli with snapper 115
    Tortellini of prawns, fish & mushrooms in seafood citrus broth 129
    Two-cheese tortellini with seared scallops & tomato & basil dressing 112
pastries *see also* pies; tarts
    Poppy seed & tuna triangles with spiced yoghurt 32
    Smoked fish puffs with garlic mayonnaise 45
pastry *see also* pastries; pies; tarts
    choux pastry 45
    cream cheese pastry for tarts 204
    flan pastry 74
pâté, smoked kahawai 48
paua/abalone *26*, 38
    Citrus paua with herbed butter 38
peanuts 119, 126, 140
pecans 72
pecorino cheese 115
pepper, peppercorns *see also* chilli; spices
    beurre blanc 160
    Black pepper market fish salad 67
    citrus & black pepper dressing 168
    Mussels grilled with peppercorns 54
    New York cut pepper 116, 138, 210, 277
    Salt & pepper squid with sweet chilli & wasabi aioli 171
Pernod
    Orange Pernod glaze 264
    Pernod cream sauce 236
pesto
    basil pesto 269
    macadamia & rocket pesto 269
    watercress pesto 177
pies *see also* pastries; tarts
    Fish pie with puff pastry 237
    Salmon & spinach filo pie 218
    Smoked fish pies 226
    Smoked fish & spinach pies 220
pimento & chive butter 270
pine nuts 269
pineapple
    Barbecued tandoori prawn & pineapple skewers with minted yoghurt 79
    Coconut & chilli seafood parcels 92
    Fish head soup 244
    Seared scallops with vanilla leek & pineapple & melon salsa 106
pipi *26*, 249
    Bouillabaisse 257
    Pipi soup, bach-style 249
    Tuatua soup 252
    Sweet & sour wok-fried crab 193
    Wok-fried black bean pipi 86
poached fish fillets 17
Poached monkfish in potato & tomato casserole 228
Poached seafood roulade, spinach & sauce vierge 68
polenta: Snapper with green pea purée & crispy shrimp polenta 184

ponzu vinaigrette 86
Poppy seed & tuna triangles with spiced
    yoghurt 32
porae *26*, 155
portobello mushrooms *see* mushrooms
potato *see also* Maori potato
    Baked white fish with Pernod cream
        sauce & potatoes 236
    Barbecued bluenose on crushed potatoes
        with caper, lemon & olive
        dressing 155
    Barbecued seafood platter with charred
        vegetables & rosemary potatoes 132
    Bouillabaisse 257
    Chargrilled maple & apple salmon steaks,
        baked potatoes & fennel slaw 148
    Fennel-crusted kingfish with olive oil-
        crushed potatoes 178
    Fishcakes topped with eggplant dip 85
    Herb-crusted fish fillets with bean &
        potato salad & salsa verde 73
    Hot-smoked broadbill with mash &
        caper sauce 215
    Hot-smoked salmon with potato cakes
        & beurre blanc 160
    mash 146, 215, 226
    Pan-fried hapuku with sautéed
        potatoes 190
    Poached monkfish in potato & tomato
        casserole 228
    potato cakes 160
    Potato & green bean salad with
        watercress pesto 177
    Scallop & potato Panang curry 225
    Seafood soup with garlic crostini 242
    Seared snapper on potato & green bean
        salad with watercress pesto 177
    Seared tuna Niçoise 174
    Smoked fish pies 226
    Warm squid salad with summer leaves &
        croutons 76
    Whole barbecue-grilled market fish
        with Greek potato mash 146
prawn, prawn cutlets, prawn meat;
    see also scampi
    Barbecued corn & prawn fritters 50
    Barbecued tandoori prawn & pineapple
        skewers with minted yoghurt 79
    Bouillabaisse 257
    Crayfish bisque with leek & prawns 256
    Crispy tiger prawns with lime &
        chilli 144
    Fettuccine with seasonal seafood, rocket
        & lemon 122
    Fish consommé 248
    Flounder paupiettes with prawns,
        spinach & lemon beurre blanc 70
    Garlic & ginger sautéed prawns with
        pumpkin soup 247
    Gratin of white fish, scallops & prawns
        with karengo 210
    Grilled Caesar salad with barbecued
        scallops & prawns 82
    Grilled prawns with tomato, feta &
        dill 150
    Jambalaya 214
    Mediterranean-style grilled scampi 144
    Mexican-style prawn cocktail 62
    Nasi goreng 119
    Open prawn wontons 98

Paella 110
Pan-fried broadbill in a saffron sauce 200
Prawn & chorizo skewers with beetroot
    & feta salad 72
Prawn, fish & corn steamed
    moneybags 36
Prawn & papaya salad with lemongrass
    dressing 102
Prawn & squid noodle box 114
Prosciutto-wrapped prawn skewers 58
Seafood & chorizo with fava beans 216
Seafood chowder 254
Seafood crêpes 97
Seafood gumbo 219
Seafood soup with garlic crostini 242
Tempura of prawn 176
Thai hot & sour prawn soup 245
Tortellini of prawns, fish & mushrooms
    in seafood citrus broth 129
Ultimate seafood mixed grill 158
Vietnamese prawn rice paper wraps 66
Wok-fried prawns with lemongrass &
    tamarind 170
prawn killer 53
    Minted lettuce scampi cups 53
    Scampi with kawakawa aioli 53
preserved lemon 115, 180, 206, 271
prosciutto
    Prosciutto-wrapped medallions of salmon
        with scallop & herb mousse 168
    Prosciutto-wrapped prawn skewers 58
pumpkin: Garlic & ginger sautéed fish
    with pumpkin soup 247

R

radicchio 73
rattails *26*
ravioli *see* pasta
raw fish *see* ceviche; gravadlax; sushi
    & sashimi
ray's bream *26*
red cod *26*
red gurnard *26*
red onion 62, 64, 88, 92, 98, 100, 110, 138
    avocado salsa 149
    Charred vegetables 132
    tropical fruit salsa 183
    Red wine risotto with sautéed squid &
        seasonal white fish 116
relish
    Grilled fish fillets with chilli jam-spiced
        eggplant relish & green beans 143
    spiced eggplant relish 143
ribaldo *26*
rice 61, 70, 92, 136, 138 *see also* risotto
    Arborio rice *see* risotto
    Crispy-skinned alfonsino with creamy
        sweetcorn & crab risotto 124
    Jambalaya 214
    Kedgeree 118
    Kingfish with a Mexican spice paste
        baked in banana leaves 212
    Nasi goreng 119
    Paella 110
    Pan-fried cod on risotto 115
    Red wine risotto with sautéed squid &
        seasonal white fish 116
    Seafood gumbo 219
    sushi rice 78

Tuatua soup 252
rice noodles *see* noodles
ricotta: Open ravioli with snapper 115
risotto
    Crispy-skinned alfonsino with creamy
        sweetcorn & crab risotto 124
    Pan-fried cod on risotto 115
    Red wine risotto with sautéed squid &
        seasonal white fish 116
rock lobster *see* crayfish
rocket 35, 162
    Fettuccine with seasonal seafood, rocket
        & lemon 122
    macadamia & rocket pesto 269
rosemary potatoes 132
roughy, orange *27*
roulade: Poached seafood roulade, spinach
    & sauce vierge 68
rubs *see* spices
ruby fish *27*
rudderfish *27*

S

saffron
    Clams with spaghetti, saffron & leek 126
    Pan-fried broadbill in a saffron sauce 200
    Seafood citrus broth 129
sage & orange barbecued mussels 150
salad *see also* salsa
    Bean & potato salad 73
    Beetroot & feta salad 72
    Black pepper market fish salad 67
    Fish ceviche 45
    Grilled Caesar salad with barbecued
        scallops & prawns 82
    Mussel, coconut & tamarind salad 104
    Potato & green bean salad with
        watercress pesto 177
    Prawn & papaya salad with lemongrass
        dressing 102
    Salad of fennel-crusted kingfish with
        orange, watercress, fennel & olives 90
    Salmon ceviche with fresh tortilla
        chips 34
    Seared scallops with vanilla leek &
        pineapple & melon salsa 106
    Seared tuna Niçoise 174
    Somen noodle salad 120
    Teriyaki salmon with somen noodle
        salad 120
    Warm squid salad with summer leaves &
        croutons 76
salmon, smoked salmon *27*, 120
    Asian herb & chilli linguine with
        marinated salmon skewers 123
    Bacon-wrapped salmon on portobello
        mushrooms 189
    Barbecued black bean salmon fillet on
        ginger & sesame vegetables 137
    Barbecued fish with hot & sour chilli
        sauce 138
    Barbecued seafood platter with charred
        vegetables & rosemary potatoes 132
    Bouillabaisse 257
    Chargrilled maple & apple salmon steaks,
        baked potatoes & fennel slaw 148
    Chenin Blanc nage with a seafood
        medley & summer vegetables 253

Eggs Benedict with salmon on kumara cakes & orange Hollandaise 199
Fish pie with puff pastry 237
Flounder paupiettes with prawns, spinach & lemon beurre blanc 70
Ginger & manuka–honey glazed hot-smoked salmon 149
Gravadlax 54
Hot-smoked salmon with potato cakes & beurre blanc 160
Kedgeree 118
Oysters & salmon in Asian broth 244
Poached seafood roulade, spinach & sauce vierge 68
Prosciutto-wrapped medallions of salmon with scallop & herb mousse 168
Salmon carpaccio 35
Salmon ceviche with fresh tortilla chips 34
Salmon & spinach filo pie 218
Salmon with caper & olive dressing 220
Seafood soup with garlic crostini 242
Smoked fish puffs with garlic mayonnaise 45
Smoked salmon, leek & beer fritters with garlic mayonnaise 101
Sushi & sashimi 78
Tea-steamed salmon with Thai red curry & coconut cream emulsion 238
Teriyaki salmon with somen noodle salad 120
Ultimate seafood mixed grill 158
Whitebait flan 74
salmon caviar: Mussel, coconut & tamarind salad 104
salmon roe: Sushi & sashimi 78
salsa 62
avocado salsa 149
green salsa 268
olive salsa 268
pineapple & melon salsa 104
salsa verde 73, 196
tomato & basil salsa 268
tomato & red onion salsa 62
tropical fruit salsa 183
Salsa al pomodoro (tomato sauce) 266
Salt & pepper squid with sweet chilli & wasabi aioli 171
sardine/pilchard 27
sashimi & sushi 78
sauce see also dipping sauce; mayonnaise; salsa
caper sauce 215
Chilli sauce 267
herb & mustard cream sauce 218
Hollandaise 74, 265
hot & sour chilli sauce 138
lemon beurre blanc 70
lemongrass sauce 61
mandarin & ginger sauce 136
Pernod cream sauce 236
saffron sauce 200
Sauce remoulade 264
Sauce tartare 264, 266
sauce vierge 68
sweet & sour sauce 193
scallops 27, 44
carpaccio 35
Chenin Blanc nage with a seafood medley & summer vegetables 253

Coconut & chilli seafood parcels 92
Gratin of white fish, scallops & prawns with karengo 210
Grilled Caesar salad with barbecued scallops & prawns 82
Market fish with butterbean purée, scallops & chorizo with salsa verde 196
Prosciutto-wrapped medallions of salmon with scallop & herb mousse 168
Scallop & goat's cheese fritters 67
Scallop & potato Panang curry 225
Seafood crêpes 97
Seafood gumbo 219
Seared scallops 44
Seared scallops with vanilla leek & pineapple & melon salsa 106
Spicy scallop & noodle soup 250
Two-cheese tortellini with seared scallops & tomato & basil dressing 112
scampi 144; see also prawns
Mediterranean-style grilled scampi 144
Minted lettuce scampi cups 53
Scampi with kawakawa aioli 53
Wok-fried, with lemongrass & tamarind 170
scorpion fish 27
Sea cucumber with sorbet 88
sea perch 27
sea urchin see kina
seafood see also fish and specific fish, shellfish
Barbecued seafood platter with charred vegetables & rosemary potatoes 132
Bouillabaisse 257
Chenin Blanc nage with a seafood medley & summer vegetables 253
Coconut & chilli seafood parcels 92
Fettuccine with seasonal seafood, rocket & lemon 122
Gratin of white fish, scallops & prawns with karengo 210
Mixed seafood & vegetable stir-fry with cashew nuts 188
Paella 110
Poached seafood roulade, spinach & sauce vierge 68
Seafood & chorizo with fava beans 216
Seafood chowder 254
Seafood crêpes 97
Seafood gumbo 219
Seafood marinade 264
Seafood soup with garlic crostini 242
Tortellini of prawns, fish & mushrooms in seafood citrus broth 129
Tuatua soup 252
Ultimate seafood mixed grill 158
Seared monkfish fillets with semi-dried tomatoes & fresh herbs 172
Seared scallops 44
Seared scallops with vanilla leek & pineapple & melon salsa 106
Seared snapper on potato & green bean salad with watercress pesto 177
Seared tuna Niçoise 174
Seared tuna rolls with seaweed salad 192
seaweed, nori, karengo, kombu
Gratin of white fish, scallops & prawns with karengo 210
Japanese crayfish soup 246
marinated seaweed salad 192

Sushi & sashimi 78
sesame seeds 86, 120, 136, 260
Ginger & sesame vegetables 137
shark, school 28
shellfish see specific shellfish; seafood
shiitake mushrooms
Crispy-skinned snapper with mushrooms, ginger & tropical fruit salsa 183
Japanese crayfish soup 246
Tortellini of prawns, fish & mushrooms in seafood citrus broth 129
shrimp: Snapper with green pea purée & crispy shrimp polenta 184
silverside 28
skate, smooth 28
skewers
Asian herb & chilli linguine with marinated salmon skewers 123
Barbecued tandoori prawn & pineapple skewers with minted yoghurt 79
Prawn & chorizo skewers with beetroot & feta salad 72
Prosciutto-wrapped prawn skewers 58
Smoked eel with mustard mousse 52
smoked fish see also fish; salmon
Fish pie with puff pastry 237
Ginger & manuka–honey glazed hot-smoked kahawai 149
Hot-smoked broadbill with mash & caper sauce 215
Hot-smoked salmon with potato cakes & beurre blanc 160
hot-smoking fish 149, 160
Kedgeree 118
smoke mix 149, 160
Smoked fish mousse 49
Smoked fish pies 226
Smoked fish puffs with garlic mayonnaise 45
Smoked fish & spinach pies 220
Smoked kahawai pâté 48
Smoked salmon, leek & beer fritters with garlic mayonnaise 101
snapper, red snapper 28, 49, 146; see also fish; smoked fish
Baked white fish with Pernod cream sauce & potatoes 236
Barbecued seafood platter with charred vegetables & rosemary potatoes 132
Barbecued sticky Chinese orange & ginger snapper parcels 154
Beer-battered fish fillets 186
Crispy-skinned snapper with mushrooms, ginger & tropical fruit salsa 183
Crispy-skinned snapper with red capsicum & fennel confit & black olive tapenade 194
Fish burgers 162
Fish ceviche 45
Fishcakes topped with eggplant dip 85
Market fish with butterbean purée, scallops & chorizo with salsa verde 196
Market fish with eggplant, tomato & mozzarella 228
Mediterranean-inspired whole baked fish 208
Open ravioli with snapper 115
Pan-fried, with sautéed potatoes 190

Seafood soup with garlic crostini 242
Seared snapper on potato & green bean
    salad with watercress pesto 177
Smoked fish & spinach pies 220
Snapper & chorizo tacos 64
Snapper on curry-spiced cauliflower
    florets with coconut cream & lychee
    foam 198
Snapper with green pea purée & crispy
    shrimp polenta 184
Whole barbecue-grilled market fish
    with Greek potato mash 146
Whole snapper steamed with ginger,
    basil & chilli 222
sole *28*, 70
somen noodles *see* noodles
sorbet: Sea cucumber with sorbet 88
soup, bisque, chowder
Chenin Blanc nage with a seafood
    medley & summer vegetables 253
Crayfish bisque with leek & prawns 256
Fish consommé 248
Fish head soup 244
Fish, tomato & lemongrass soup 250
Garlic & ginger sautéed fish with
    pumpkin soup 247
Mussel chowder 254
Oysters & salmon in Asian broth 244
Pipi soup, bach-style 249
Pumpkin soup 247
Seafood chowder 254
Seafood citrus broth 129
Seafood soup with garlic crostini 242
Spicy scallop & noodle soup 250
Thai hot & sour prawn soup 245
Tuatua soup 252
sour cream: Smoked eel with mustard
    mousse 52
sowfish *28*
spaghetti *see* pasta
spanner crab *see* crab
spiced eggplant relish 143
spices
Asian spices 140
Cajun spice mix 146, 156, 160, 215,
    219, 261
chermoula 261
Chinese five spice 134, 154
curry paste 225, 232
dukkah 132, 260
fennel spice mix 90, 178
Mexican spice paste 212
Moroccan spice 158, 180
North African 159
pepper *see* pepper
spices for smoking fish 149, 160
Spicy scallop & noodle soup 250
spicy yoghurt & harissa dressing 263
spinach 39, 98, 129, 178, 190, 236, 244
Flounder paupiettes with prawns,
    spinach & lemon beurre blanc 70
Poached seafood roulade, spinach &
    sauce vierge 68
Salmon & spinach filo pie 218
Smoked fish & spinach pies 220
spinach yoghurt dressing 263
sprat *28*
squid *29*, 76
Barbecue-seared five-spice squid with
    wasabi aioli 134

Barbecued chilli squid with Asian spices
    & green beans 140
Barbecued seafood platter with charred
    vegetables & rosemary potatoes 132
Chenin Blanc nage with a seafood
    medley & summer vegetables 253
Coconut & chilli seafood parcels 92
Fettuccine with seasonal seafood, rocket
    & lemon 122
Paella 110
Prawn & squid noodle box 114
Red wine risotto with sautéed squid &
    seasonal white fish 116
Salt & pepper squid with sweet chilli &
    wasabi aioli 171
Seafood & chorizo with fava beans 216
Warm squid salad with summer leaves &
    croutons 76
steamed fish 16
Tea-steamed salmon 238
Whole snapper steamed with ginger,
    basil & chilli 222
stew
Bouillabaisse 257
Fish & tomato Spanish-style stew 214
stock *see* dashi; fish stock; soup
sushi 78
Sushi & sashimi 78
sushi rice 78
Sweet & sour wok-fried crab 193
swordfish *29*

T

tacos: Snapper & chorizo tacos 64
tamarind
Mussel, coconut & tamarind salad 104
Wok-fried prawns with lemongrass &
    tamarind 170
tandoori paste 79
Barbecued tandoori prawn & pineapple
    skewers with minted yoghurt 79
tapenade 194
Crispy-skinned snapper with red
    capsicum & fennel confit & black
    olive tapenade 194
tarakihi *29*, 49, 198, 208
Baked white fish with Pernod cream
    sauce & potatoes 236
Barbecued tarakihi on crushed potatoes
    with caper, lemon & olive
    dressing 155
Beer-battered fish fillets 186
Fish burgers 162
Fishcakes topped with eggplant dip 85
Market fish with eggplant, tomato &
    mozzarella 228
Mediterranean-inspired whole baked
    fish 208
Seafood soup with garlic crostini 242
Smoked fish & spinach pies 220
tarragon
tarragon butter 270
tarragon & mustard aioli 224
tartare
sauce tartare 266
tartare butter 270
tuna tartare 35
tarts, flans *see also* pies
Fish tartlets with fresh herbs 204

Monkfish, tomato & feta tarts 62
Whitebait flan 74
Tataki of tuna 86
Tea-steamed salmon with Thai red curry &
    coconut cream emulsion 238
Tempura of prawn 176
teppanyaki dipping sauce 266
tequila: Mexican-style prawn cocktail 62
teriyaki sauce 120
Teriyaki salmon with somen noodle
    salad 120
Thai hot & sour prawn soup 245
Thai red curry 271
Mussels steamed in Thai red curry with
    citrus 234
Pumpkin soup 247
Thai red curry & coconut cream
    emulsion 238
Thai red curry paste (nam prik gaeng
    phed) 271
Thai red curry with fish 216
Thai vegetable rice noodles 126
tiger prawns *see* prawns
tomato *see also* cherry tomato
Fish ceviche 45
Fish, tomato & lemongrass soup 250
Fish & tomato Spanish-style stew 214
Grilled prawns with tomato, feta &
    dill 150
Jambalaya 214
Kasbah mussels with tomatoes,
    coriander, olives & capsicum 159
Market fish with eggplant, tomato &
    mozzarella 228
Mexican-style prawn cocktail 62
Paella 110
Poached monkfish in potato & tomato
    casserole 228
salsa al pomodoro 266
Sea cucumber with sorbet 88
tomato & basil dressing 112, 178
tomato & basil salsa 268
Ultimate seafood mixed grill 158
warm tomato vinaigrette 262
tomato, dried/semi-dried/sun-dried
    100, 206
Bouillabaisse 257
dried tomato & basil butter 270
Monkfish, tomato & feta tarts 62
Seared monkfish fillets with semi-dried
    tomatoes & fresh herbs 172
sun-dried tomato aioli 189
tortellini *see also* pasta
Tortellini of prawns, fish & mushrooms
    in seafood citrus broth 129
Two-cheese tortellini with seared scallops
    & tomato & basil dressing 112
tortillas, corn tortillas 34, 272
Kingfish with a Mexican spice paste
    baked in banana leaves 212
Salmon ceviche with fresh tortilla
    chips 34, 62
Snapper & chorizo tacos 64
tortilla chips 34
trevally *29*
Ginger & manuka-honey glazed hot-
    smoked trevally 149
Trevally baked in a citrus salt crust with
    mustard & tarragon aioli 224
tropical fruit salsa 183

trumpeter *29*
Tuatua soup 252
tuna *29*, 40
    Fennel-crusted, with olive oil-crushed
        potatoes 178
    Market fish with eggplant, tomato &
        mozzarella 228
    Parmesan & olive wafer stack with
        seared tuna 40
    Poppy seed & tuna triangles with spiced
        yoghurt 32
    Seared tuna Niçoise 174
    Seared tuna rolls with seaweed salad 192
    Sushi & sashimi 78
    Tataki of tuna 86
turbot *29*
Two-cheese tortellini with seared scallops
    & tomato & basil dressing 112
tzatziki 100

U

Ultimate seafood mixed grill 158

V

vanilla
    Seared scallops with vanilla leek &
        pineapple & melon salsa 106
    smoke mix 149
vegetables *see also specific vegetables*
    Charred vegetables 132
    Chenin Blanc nage with a seafood
        medley & summer vegetables 253
    Barbecued black bean salmon fillet on
        ginger & sesame vegetables 137

Mixed seafood & vegetable stir-fry with
    cashew nuts 188
Seafood soup with garlic crostini 242
Thai vegetable rice noodles 126
velouté
    Fish velouté 249
    Smoked fish mousse 49
Vietnamese prawn rice paper wraps 66
vinaigrette *see* dressing
vincotto reduction 264
vodka: Kina Bloody Mary 50

W

wafers, Parmesan 40
warehou *29*
Warm squid salad with summer leaves &
    croutons 76
wasabi
    Barbecue-seared five-spice squid with
        wasabi aioli 134
    Salt & pepper squid with sweet chilli &
        wasabi aioli 171
    Sushi & sashimi 78
    sweet chilli & wasabi aioli 171
water chestnut 98
watercress
    Mussel chowder 254
    Seared snapper on potato & green bean
        salad with watercress pesto 177
Whelks in vinaigrette 88
white fish *see* fish *and specific fish*, e.g.
    gurnard; hapuku; hoki, ling, monkfish,
    snapper, tarakihi
White fish with chilli, Mexican herbs &
    green olives 89

whitebait
    Whitebait flan 74
    Whitebait fritters 80
Whole barbecue-grilled market fish with
    Greek potato mash 146
Whole pan-seared flounder 174
Whole snapper steamed with ginger, basil
    & chilli 222
wine 18
    Chenin Blanc nage with a seafood
        medley & summer vegetables 253
    Red wine risotto with sautéed squid &
        seasonal white fish 116
Wok-fried black bean pipi 86
Wok-fried prawns with lemongrass &
    tamarind 170
wontons, wonton wrappers
    Open prawn wontons 98
    Prawn, fish & corn steamed
        moneybags 36
    Tortellini of prawns, fish & mushrooms
        in seafood citrus broth 129
    Two-cheese tortellini with seared
        scallops 112

Y

yeast batter 260
yoghurt
    dill yoghurt 209
    minted yoghurt dipping sauce 79
    Poppy seed & tuna triangles with spiced
        yoghurt 32
    spicy yoghurt & harissa dressing 263
    spinach yoghurt dressing 263
    tzatziki 100

Acknowledgements

The Auckland Seafood School would like to acknowledge the chefs who made this book possible – particularly the wonderfully talented core team of John Campbell, Colin Doyle, Mark Dronjak, Marco Edwardes, Petra New and Steve Roberts. Their ongoing support and passion for the Auckland Seafood School is greatly appreciated. Thank you to our great kitchen and administration team at the school. Your dedication and support make all the difference. Thank you also to chef Jason McGeorge for providing several recipes.

The Auckland Seafood School would also like to thank photographer Sean Shadbolt and stylist Athena Sommerfeld for the beautiful food photography, photographer Jason Burgess for his enthusiasm and stunning lifestyle photography, Graeme Sinclair – an incredible industry advocate, and Sandee Sinclair for her photographs. Finally, thank you to Sanford Limited and Seafood NZ Limited for their information and ongoing support of the Auckland Seafood School.
www.seafood.co.nz

PENGUIN BOOKS
Published by the Penguin Group
Penguin Group (NZ), 67 Apollo Drive, Rosedale,
Auckland 0632, New Zealand (a division of Pearson New Zealand Ltd)

Penguin Books Ltd, Registered Offices: 80 Strand, London, WC2R 0RL, England

First published by Penguin Group (NZ), 2013
10 9 8 7 6 5 4 3

Designed and typeset by Jenny Haslimeier, © Penguin Group (NZ)
Food photography by Sean Shadbolt
Food styling by Athena Sommerfeld
Food photography props: stylist's and chefs' own plus Ballarini white frying pans and Luigi Bormioli wine glasses
Photography on pages 2, 5 (except middle right), 7, 8, 10, 13 (except top and bottom middle), 19, 20, 273, 287 and 288 by Jason Burgess
Photography on pages 5 (middle right) and 13 (top and bottom middle) by Sandee Sinclair
Species photographs on pages 21–29 and 'Did you know?' information courtesy of Seafood New Zealand Limited
Prepress by Image Centre Ltd
Printed in China by RR Donnelley Asia Printing Solutions Limited

ISBN 978-0-143-56939-8

A catalogue record for this book is available
from the National Library of New Zealand.

www.penguin.co.nz